Days on the Water

A John D. S. and Aida C. Truxall Book

Days on the Water

The Angling Tradition
in Pennsylvania

Mike Sajna

University of Pittsburgh Press

For BC and Bob "Tug" Dragovich,
two of my best fishing companions.

Published by the University of Pittsburgh Press, Pittsburgh, Pa. 15261
Copyright © 1999, University of Pittsburgh Press
All rights reserved
Manufactured in the United States of America
Printed on acid-free paper
10 9 8 7 6 5 4 3 2 1

ISBN 0-8229-4039-6

A CIP catalog record for this book is available from the Library of
Congress and the British Library

Contents

Part 4 ⟿ Dog Days

PART 1

Cabin Fever

A Twenty-Three-Pound Grasshopper

"**F**ARMER SHOOTS TWENTY-THREE-POUND GRASS-HOPPER!" screams the headline on the tabloid in the convenience store. Under the headline, a grainy black-and-white photograph shows a simple-faced rube in baggy pants. He is holding the hind legs of a creature that looks as if it just crawled out of a Japanese science fiction movie from the 1950s, the kind of movie where the characters' mouths are never quite in sync with the sound and the fate of the Earth hangs in the balance as some monster approaches a nuclear power station outside Tokyo.

While I wait for the worn-looking blonde woman ahead of me to buy a list of lottery numbers, I reach down and pick up the tabloid. Inside, the story is about a farmer in New Zealand who found the grasshopper perched on the seat of his tractor. At first he thought his mind was playing tricks, but the next afternoon he spotted the creature clinging to a corn stalk. He knew he wasn't seeing things this time because "the damn thing spit a full quart of 'tobacco' juice and hit me square in the face." The following morning, the farmer found the grasshopper polishing off a corn stalk and shot it with his .30/30 Winchester.

The story is the first in years that has made me pick up a tabloid. The last story was about how the dinosaurs had been driven into extinction by Martian big game hunters. I imagine the grasshopper floating high on the choppy blue waters of

Montana's Madison River. I see gigantic trout rising, taking mouthfuls out of the creature's sides. I wonder if my nine-weight salmon rod might be heavy enough to fish a fly the size of that grasshopper.

Lost in the absurdity of the story and my own fantasy I drift off, and when my turn comes at the cash register I have to be prodded into action by the girl behind the counter. Embarrassed at being caught reading the story, I fumble the tabloid back in its rack and pay for my newspaper and milk. Then I duck out the door into the parking lot. Traffic hums by on Route 30. The sky is a high, drifting-cloud blue that says April. I think I must be slipping, for sure, to daydream about a story so stupid as a four-foot grasshopper. An overload of work, bad weather, other distractions, clearly I've been indoors too long. I need to go fishing.

Being self-employed has plenty of disadvantages (there's no one else to blame for failure and no paid vacations), but it has some wonderful advantages—no bosses, and a schedule that usually can be manipulated. When I pull out onto Route 30 near my home in Irwin, I am laughing at my friends stuck behind desks and inside factories. I can't wait to rub it in that I spent the day on the water.

Loyalhanna Creek in eastern Westmoreland County is the nearest trout stream to my home, with a special regulation project open to fishing prior to the official start of Pennsylvania's trout season in mid-April. It lies for me at the end of a nearly unbroken thirty-mile chain of malls, car dealerships, shopping centers, fast food restaurants, supermarkets, discount outlets, motels, and appliance stores. To reach it, I must contend with almost one traffic light per mile, and the number seems to be growing every year.

In the early afternoon the trip is usually not too bad, basically a race to beat the red lights. Except on Fridays. No sooner do I pull onto Route 30 than I find myself caught in a line of cars carrying visibly edgy people who have fled work early to stretch their weekends. The sight reminds me of past lives spent in offices and makes me shiver in fear. Then I spot the first hints of green on the shrubs growing in the road cut near Norwin Junior High School East. I pass through the cut every day, but my mind is usually elsewhere. This is the first time I've noticed the fragile color. It is exciting.

The green lasts only a few seconds before commerce claims its due again, and I am caught at a red light between two shopping centers. Glancing up at the multiplex marquee at the entrance to one of the shopping centers, I notice that a Teenage Mutant Ninja Turtle movie is playing. A flash of guilt strikes me. Norwin teachers are having an in-service day. School is out. BC probably would love to see the Turtles—but the draw of trout is more powerful than her giggle. The guilt passes. We've already talked on the phone. Maybe we can go to the movies tomorrow, I tell myself.

The shrubs in the road cut make me wonder if the mountains have started to turn green yet, when the radio picks up the opening chords of "Purple Haze." I have never particularly cared for Jimi Hendrix, but right now the song is liberating. It reminds me of college—fifteen-cent beer at the Polish Club, parties, girls, marijuana at twenty dollars an ounce. Now, I hear it sells for $250 a ounce. I remember friends who used to get high and go fishing. They said it made the experience better, but I never understood how. The one time I tried fishing, high, it ruined my concentration and I felt angry at myself for wasting a precious day on the water.

There are only three cars in the nature trail parking lot along Loyalhanna Creek, across from the town of Ligonier. The sight thrills me with visions of solitude. My thrill is enhanced when a fisherman—dressed impeccably in matching neoprene waders, shoes, vest, hat, rod, and reel—appears and unlocks the trunk of an expensive Swedish car. We nod to each other but do not speak. I am too anxious to get on the water to want to make small talk. Hurriedly, I yank my wading bag from the trunk of my car and pull out my waders.

Dressed, I stuff the wading bag back in the trunk and take my reel from its case and rod from its tube. My excitement grows at the feel of them and it's a struggle to fit everything together. I slam the trunk shut, nod to the fisherman, and hurry across the parking lot.

Although trout season has not yet opened, the path leading to the water is a sty of muddy boot prints and I'm fretting that maybe the empty parking lot was just an illusion and really the stream is packed with anglers. Since there are a lot of places to park along the Loyalhanna, it sometimes happens that way. Then a second angler appears heading for the parking lot and my spirits rise.

At the swinging bridge, I have to pause for a moment in awe. I can't believe how good the water looks. It is lower and clearer than I ever would have dared expect for April. I slip on my polarized glasses and begin looking for fish. None show in the shallow water below me, but this is not surprising. The trench along the opposite bank is the holding water. I pull out my thermometer and climb down the bank. The air temperature is about fifty degrees, so I expect the water to be somewhere in the low forties, maybe upper thirties, definitely not the eight degrees that shows on the thermometer.

"That can't be right," I tell myself. Then I notice a gap in the red. I shake the thermometer, beat it against my leg, and dip it back into the stream, but the red stays separated and nothing changes. Puzzled, I tuck the instrument back in my vest, walk downstream to the tail of the pool, slip into the water, and dig out the small fly box that holds my Green Weenies.

Named for the green plastic hot dogs used to cheer the Pirates on to victory in the 1960 World Series, the Green Weenie is simply a piece of chartreuse chenille wrapped around a hook. Since it bears no resemblance to any known aquatic insect, many match-the-hatch anglers refuse to use it—or soothe their qualms by pretending it is an inchworm. I'll admit, it really is a lure, but it works, and I need to catch a fish. Last year on Conewago Creek outside Gettysburg, I caught sixteen trout on it and missed another half-dozen within two hours.

It is exactly 1:40 P.M. when I see my first rise of the year. It dimples the surface tight against the rock wall along the opposite bank. The sight takes my breath away. When the fish shows again, the idea of dry fly fishing enters my mind, and the thought is reinforced when a mayfly dun floats past. The fly is too far away to identify, but I guess it's a Blue Dun, an early season fly I've encountered before on the Loyalhanna. I wonder if there may be more on the way and if that's what brought up the fish.

I am still contemplating the situation, when the trout rises a third time and the urge to go dry takes over. I give up the Green Weenie for an Adams, as a second fish dimples the surface a couple of feet above the first. I think it's probably a chub, but I shoot a cast in its direction anyway and connect.

Skunk Cabbage Fever

Monopolized by images of trout rising to dry flies, I can't wait to get back on the water, but Saturday comes with six inches of snow. If there is that much in the suburbs, I know the mountains are probably blanketed. Sunday is Easter, with all its family obligations. When Monday finally arrives, I watch helpless as the sky switches on and off, sunny to overcast, until I decide it is smarter to stay home and work. When it starts to rain and then snow I feel good about my choice. But concentration can be hard to muster against the thought of fishing, and the day passes in a general sense of alternating distraction and forced labor, and I find release only when I sit down at the tying vice.

Fly tying is far from my favorite activity. I lack the patience to turn it into art. I do it mainly because it is cheaper than buying flies and allows me to adapt to conditions, which is usually the way I tie—when a hatch is on that I can't match with whatever is already in one of my fly boxes, or something is working that I don't have in one of my boxes. Such laziness means I prefer simple fly patterns, particularly those requiring only minor changes in size and color to resemble about ten thousand different insects:

flies like the Hare's Ear, Adams, and Sulphur. The fish don't know or care that I've spent only a couple of minutes, not an hour, tying each one or that they don't imitate any specific insect. To the fish, my flies simply look like a meal. The only time a fish is caught anyway is when it makes a mistake. Unless a trout is tuned in to a hatch, I've found them just as likely to take a Pheasant Tail Soft-Hackle as an exact imitation of *Brachycentrus fuliginosus* or *Ganonema americana*. Even during a hatch, they sometimes will hit one of my impressionistic patterns and not take a match just because my fly is different. Since I don't worry about losing flies so easy to tie, I believe I catch more fish on my simple patterns than many anglers do with their elaborate creations because I'm not afraid to cast into tight spots.

Occasionally I do like to experiment, though, especially with British and Irish patterns: Daddy Longlegs, Straddlebugs, Goslings, Sedges. I like their colors, their design, and the way they sometimes can fool American trout that have seen practically every fly used on this side of the Atlantic. Then there are those stories behind them, too, tales like the one of Michael Rogan's Fiery Brown. Rogan was Ireland's great nineteenth-century tier, and for years nobody could figure out how he dyed the materials used in the Fiery Brown, his most famous fly. The secret turned out to be stale jack-ass urine, which, according to E. J. Malone in *Irish Trout and Salmon Flies*, is still used today by Scottish weavers to dye tweeds.

At the moment I am not so ambitious, though. Peace comes as an emerging nymph. It is a pattern I've been procrastinating over for a decade, the one that uses a tiny piece of panty hose to form a ball over the wing case and trap air that makes it float just beneath the surface like a nymph about to hatch. When I dig through my boxes of tying materials, I can't find a piece of panty hose. I decide to improvise with clippings of gray and brown poly yarn.

As I knock off variations of the pattern using Hare's Ear and Zug Bug bodies, every trout I've ever seen taking emergers comes back to me. As in one of those videos in which a famous angler casually points out trout feeding on emergers and then ties one on and begins catching fish after fish, I see myself fooling every trout that has ever frustrated me in such a manner. They fall as helpless as fish in a barrel, ducks on a pond, sheep going to market, and every other cliché.

Although it never feels that way at the time, pushing on often produces something usable. In the morning I find the story from the day before only needs a little polishing, which takes a couple of hours. I once again begin to think about fishing, which this time leads to guilt. Work has gone so well, I wonder if it is better to stay home and continue working. I have never quite been able to rid myself of an upbringing that stressed the importance of work. Time off during the week often comes with guilt.

Then I recall a letter I recently stumbled across that Benjamin Franklin wrote about the Indians and the utter lack of success the colonists were having in civilizing them:

> The proneness of human Nature to a life of ease, of freedom from care and labour appears strongly in the little success that has hitherto attended every attempt to civilize our American Indians in their present way of living, almost all their Wants are supplied by the spontaneous Productions of Nature, with the addition of very little labour, if hunting and fishing may indeed be called labour . . . they visit us frequently, and see the advantages that Arts, Sciences, and compact Society procure us, they are not deficient in natural understanding and yet they have never shewn an Inclination to change their manner of life for ours, or to learn our Arts. . . . They have few but natural wants and those easily supplied. But with us are infinite Artificial wants, no less craving than those of Nature, and much more difficult to satisfy.

I need to be uncivilized, I think, and switch off my computer.

When I reach Loyalhanna Creek, I am pleasantly surprised by how clear and steady it is flowing after all the rain and snow of the past few days. I spot a caddis fly bouncing off the surface, and then a palomino trout holding near the center of the stream. Bob Runk, a friend from the Fly Fishers Club of Pittsburgh, once called the palomino's orange-gold color "an abomination of nature" for the unnatural way it makes the fish stand out. Personally, I suspect that palominos are brain dead, since I've often seen them rise to strike bubbles and twigs while ignoring live insects floating nearby.

My contemplation of the palomino is broken when a dead rainbow floats past. There is no waste in nature. It will be used by a raccoon, an opossum, a skunk, or at the very least, the microbes in the soil, but the sight still saddens me, and it saddens me more each year. I watch the rainbow until it tumbles out of sight with the current and then turn upstream.

The known being more comfortable than the unknown, I am tempted to return to the spot I fished on Friday. Then I realize I haven't seen much of the Loyalhanna so far this year, and I head downstream. Nobody is in sight as I slip into the water below a lump of concrete from a long-gone bridge and I smile at the prospects of having the whole place to myself. A fish rises just ahead of the concrete, stirring thoughts of a repeat performance of my opening day, but before I can make a cast another fisherman appears about fifty feet above me. Annoyed he should choose a spot so close to me when the stream is otherwise empty, I consider moving on, but I know from experience that the water around the concrete always holds trout—and one of them is rising. I push the intrusion out of my mind, tie on an Adams, and cast toward the spot where the fish last showed.

Unlike three days ago, this fish has no interest in my fly. After a dozen or so passes without any reaction, I remember the caddis fly I saw bouncing across the surface and switch to an Elk Hair Caddis. When that fails, I think it is time to try one of my new emergers. When this too fails, I am left to rummage through my fly boxes.

Lost in the problem of the trout, I am taken aback when I glance up to find a scant fifteen feet separating me from the only other fisherman on the water. I am totally surprised at his arrogance and lack of manners. As he continues to cast and move closer, I can only stare in disbelief. When he finally decides to get out of the stream, he is so close I can touch him with my rod.

Although such behavior is nothing unusual on Pennsylvania's often crowded trout streams, it is always somehow unexpected— at least to me—in special regulation projects where anglers are generally thought to be more conscious of sportsmanship. I've never known how to handle such a lack of manners. Certain friends of mine would resort to words, rocks, even fists, if anybody crowded them in such a way on empty water, but a stream to me has always been a place to leave behind the aggressions of daily life. I can never quite make up my mind what to do in these situations. Rather than bring the world to the stream by telling off the slob, I usually move on.

This time, when the fisherman reenters the water less than ten feet downstream and begins casting to the spot I am fishing, I feel it is too much. I tie on a threadbare Pheasant Tail and cast at his line hoping he will say something, but he completely ignores me and continues to fish as if I don't exist. I'm trying hard to catch his line but he always manages to sneak it past me—until I realize I am allowing daily life to take over. Angry at myself for sinking to his level, I reel in my line and splash my way out of the pool up onto the bank. Although experience says I've done the right thing, the boy in me who grew up in a western Pennsylvania coal-mining patch still wants to turn around and hurl rocks into the water in front of him—or worse.

I am still mumbling to myself about his ignorance when a slash of bright green in the middle of a dark seasonal pool catches my eye. Like the first rising trout, the first skunk cabbage of the season is one of the most thrilling sights for me. This is spring made real. Few people know it, but the skunk cabbage produces heat when it is pollinating. For a short time, its internal temperature can be as much as thirty degrees warmer than the temperature of the surrounding air, warm enough to melt the snow around it. The plant in front of me is beyond that stage, but just the sight of its tender green melts my anger. Then I see a bouquet of daffodils growing along the bank. Their yellow and green is dazzling amid the dead dark browns of the forest floor. I walk closer to better admire them and, then, look up to find a male mallard standing proud, every feather perfectly groomed, on a gravel bar and a kingfisher diving for a minnow. The sights suddenly make the entire day a success, even without a single fish to my credit.

Genesis

Somewhere around 600 million years ago, the land that would become Pennsylvania lay at the bottom of a shallow sea in approximately the same location as Brazil. It was a mostly flat piece of underwater real estate, comparable to the continental shelf found off the East Coast today. In its waters was an abundance of algae, sand, and lime mud, a primordial ooze created by eroded limestone and the remains of sea life. Although there were fluctuations in the sea level over the centuries, the situation remained more or less constant for 150 million years, when the Earth's plates began to move closer together.

Until about 450 million years ago, Africa and North America were moving apart and there was a series of volcanic islands much like Japan and the Philippines off the coast of North America. Roughly 430 million years ago, the movement of the Earth's plates reversed, and Africa and North America began to drift toward each other. The islands of the proto–Atlantic Ocean were forced into North America, creating the mountains of southeastern Pennsylvania and the Appalachian Basin inland. This event was followed, approximately 90 million years later, by a collision between Europe and North America that forced the Appalachian Basin upward and lifted about 95 percent of Pennsylvania above water for the first time.

These events were only preludes to what occurred some 250

million years ago when Africa and North America met head-on near Philadelphia. This collision, among other things, pushed into being a tremendous mountain range that stretches across nearly half the globe. This range became known as the Atlas Mountains, in Africa; as the Caledonian Mountains, in Great Britain, Greenland, and Scandinavia; and as the Appalachians, in North America. They were as high as the Rockies, as high as the Himalayas. They were so high, their peaks were permanently covered with glaciers. Pennsylvania's Allegheny Mountains are but the nubs of the original Appalachians, worn down by aeons of rain, wind, and snow.

When Africa and North America collided, the Appalachians arose in a jumble along fractures in the Earth's crust. Since water always seeks the path of least resistance, the rain and snow running off the mountains took to the fractures, carrying off sediment in a wedge-shaped pattern across central and western Pennsylvania. Many of those paths are the basis for Pennsylvania's present river and stream system. This does not mean the rivers and streams are in the same beds as they were 250 million years ago; erosion, later uplifts in the Earth's surface, and changing sea levels have caused the state's waterways to run faster or slower over the ages and their paths to shift back and forth, up and down.

Fractures in the Earth's crust also are the reason that water gaps or cuts in the mountains such as the Delaware Water Gap in Monroe County dot the state. They are why meandering streams (more the norm in flat, open country than mountainous lands like Pennsylvania) can be found in deep valleys around places like Hyner and Lock Haven in Clinton County; why the tributary streams of the state's six major watersheds (Ohio, Potomac, Delaware, Susquehanna, Erie, and Ontario) are sometimes only separated by a hill or two; and why, in a broad geological sense, streams and rivers as distant as the Potomac and Ohio—and the Little Juniata River and Oil Creek—lie all in a line, even though they drain into different watersheds.

The collision of Africa and North America also created the Cumberland Valley's limestone streams in south central Pennsylvania. When the collision pushed the Appalachian Mountains into being, the valley was squeezed, its limestone deposits compacted under unimaginable pressure between the new mountains to the west and the old mountains around Philadelphia. In the state's relatively wet climate, the limestone dissolved, water began flowing through its fractures, and the Letort, the Yellow Breeches, Big Spring, Falling Springs, and the rest of the state's limestone streams were born.

Life on Earth is generally believed to have originated in the oceans. To live in a dry environment, organisms first had to develop special water-conserving mechanisms. Before these evolutionary changes, water had distinct advantages for supporting primitive life forms: the chemical processes of life depend upon the presence of water within the tissues, and organisms need salts within their cells to carry on the alchemy of life. In Pennsylvania, fossils of lungfish, sharks, fish scales, and spines have been found in limestone and shale deposits dating back from 345 million to 395 million years ago. Although evidence is limited, the earliest ancestors of the modern *Salmoniformes,* an order that appears on every continent and throughout the seas of the world and contains some of the most important game and commercial fishes, probably first appeared about 100 million years ago. Members of the order include trout, salmon, pickerel, smelts, char, northern pike, whitefish, and muskellunge.

It was the evolution of an anadromous life cycle, in which spawning takes place in freshwater and maturity is spent in the sea, that played one of the most important roles in the *Salmoniforme*'s wide distribution. Migratory behavior during periods of marine growth permitted members of the order to extend their range by exploring the perimeters of the oceans and entering river systems such as the Delaware and the Susquehanna. Once in these new waters, the *Salmoniformes*—because of volcanic, glacial, climatic, and other activities that either left them trapped or provided them with a more suitable habitat than they had left behind—evolved into entirely freshwater species.

Among them were the brook trout (which is not a true trout at all, but a char) and the lake trout. The brook trout's original range was limited to the Atlantic drainage system from the Hudson Straits in Canada, south to the mountains of Georgia and South Carolina. Good populations were found in all the suitable habitat in between, as well as in the Appalachian headwaters of the Ohio and streams draining into the Great Lakes. Its western limits were the rivers draining into the Hudson Bay from Manitoba and the Northwest Territories of Canada. "The species we have that are native is the brook trout," says Dr. Edwin Cooper, retired professor of zoology at Penn State University and the author of *Fishes of Pennsylvania*. "And there are probably a couple of places in the state where there were native lake trout. Harveys Lake probably had an original population and there was another lake up in the Poconos. The Great Lakes always had lake trout, too."

The collision of Europe and North America between 345 million and 395 million years ago explains the numerous similarities between the fish populations of Europe and North America. Millions of years of evolution have turned many of these fish into different species, but the same families are present on both continents. Pennsylvania today is home to no less than 159 different species of fish. Of that number, 119 are strictly freshwater and 40, such as the shad and the sculpin, are salt-tolerant or freshwater representatives of marine groups. According to Cooper: "What we have essentially came from freshwater origins and is closely associated with Europe and Asia. . . . Five families, pikes, mudminnows, minnows, suckers and perches, contribute eighty-one species to our fauna."

Pennsylvania has three definite patterns of distribution of fish populations, centering around the Delaware, Susquehanna, and Ohio river basins. The Ohio system is the richest of the three, according to Cooper, containing over 150 different species of fish. It is followed by the Susquehanna with over 100 different species, and finally the Delaware with 30 different species. The Ohio basin holds a greater variety of fish than the Susquehanna and Delaware systems combined, because of glaciation. When the glaciers scoured their way south out of Canada into northern Pennsylvania about 500,000 years ago, and again about 15,000 years ago, they altered the climate to the point where it was no longer hospitable to most species of fish then living in the state's waterways. To survive the changed conditions, fish headed downstream. Those in the Ohio basin had practically the entire Mississippi River drainage in which to find a haven; whereas the fish in the Susquehanna had only the Chesapeake Bay and the Potomac River, and those in the Delaware had only the brackish water of Delaware Bay and the Atlantic Ocean, environments totally unsuitable to the majority of species living in the state when the glaciers arrived.

During the Ice Age, West Virginia, Tennessee, Kentucky, northern Alabama, Georgia, and the Carolinas became one vast fish nursery. So many species fled south into the waters of these states that even today they hold the bulk of the nation's fish species. When the glaciers retreated and the climate once again turned favorable, the fish in these havens moved back up the Ohio to repopulate the waters of western Pennsylvania. Similarly, species in the Chesapeake Bay region headed back up the Susquehanna. Few fish returned from the Delaware Bay and the Atlantic Ocean to repopulate the Delaware, but the Delaware basin's thirty different species are more than those found in the entire state of Maine, where the glaciers left only about twenty-five species of fish. "But if you take game fishes, you get all mixed up," Cooper points out, "because they've been spreading game fish around ever since 1870. The muskie has been spread everywhere, the northern pike has been spread practically everywhere. All the trout, if they were originally somewhere else, now they are all over. The bass has been spread everywhere from Australia to Europe."

Banquets and Bible for Anglers

'For the seriously afflicted, angling banquets are as much a part of the cabin fever phase of the fishing season as that restless, gnawing urge to abandon work and family for the slightest possibility of hooking a couple of lethargic trout. These angling banquets come in two basic types with a good amount of crossover in attendance.

The first variety is a rather understated forum, at which mostly upscale anglers gather in the carpeted banquet room of a nice hotel or restaurant to dine on chicken cordon bleu or prime rib, view a slide show by some famous angler, and exchange views on tackle, streams, and flies. Dressed in coats and ties, most anglers at banquets of the first variety drink cocktails. They sprinkle their conversations with anecdotes about the Madison, the Yellowstone, Henrys Fork, Bow, Beaverkill, Christmas Island, and other far-flung waters. They study intently the raffle prizes offered to raise money for the sponsoring club's causes, then open their checkbooks and purchase long strips of tickets. Although there is enough laughter and joking to inspire a quote by Izaak Walton, everybody remains essentially under control.

The second type of banquet is a somewhat more casual affair. Many of these anglers come from neighboring small towns and have been friends for years. This type of banquet usually takes place in the uncarpeted hall of some fraternal or veterans organization, the Sons of Italy, American Legion, Veterans of Foreign Wars. Speakers could be anybody from nationally known fishing celebrities to local boys who like to carry a camera along when they are on the stream.

While the people at this second type of banquet may know just as much about fishing as those at the first type, their knowledge is more likely spiced with anecdotes from waters named Mill Creek, Spring Creek, or Buffalo Creek than Boca Chimehuin or the North Island. Their attire includes coats and ties, but also jeans and sweaters, and a few silly fish ties. Like fishermen at the other type of banquet, they also buy long strips of raffle tickets, but they usually pay in cash and are not so reserved when viewing the evening's prizes. Occasionally, somebody can be seen on his knees praying to win the grand prize rod and reel. Dinner is usually stuffed chicken breast or stuffed pork chop. Their cocktails are beer, or maybe whiskey and sours. As the evening wears on, prizewinners are greeted with boos and howls; once in a while somebody walks across the floor on their hands.

Every area of the country has its own fair share of both types of fishing clubs. Among the most unusual to be found anywhere, however, are the Fly Fishers Club of Harrisburg, Pennsylvania, and its offspring, the Fly Fishers Club of Pittsburgh. Their eccentricities start with the fact that they require absolutely nothing of their members. They have no bylaws, no elected officers, no dues, no treasury, and no membership requirements. They are anarchy at its finest. Anglers attending the Fly Fishers Club of Harrisburg's annual dinner for the first time are simply asked to stand and are then pronounced members for life. The Fly Fishers Club of Pittsburgh is even less formal. Anybody who shows up at one of its meetings automatically becomes a member. They are not even asked to stand.

The idea for the Harrisburg club originated in 1946 with two of Pennsylvania's best-known and most revered fishermen: Charlie Fox, author of *This Wonderful World of Trout* and *Rising Trout,* and his angling partner Vince Marinaro, author of *In the Ring of the Rise* and *A Modern Dry-Fly Code,* which is arguably the most influential fishing book of the twentieth century. According to S. R. Slaymaker, in "The Fly Fishers Club of Harrisburg," Fox and Marinaro were members of a Harrisburg area sportsmen's club dominated by deer hunters when they became bored by the club's long formal meetings and they dropped out. One day not too long afterward, Fox suggested to Marinaro that they form a new club centered around fly fishing. Marinaro liked the idea and borrowed the name from the Fly Fishers Club of London, a group he greatly admired.

Although the new club was formed ostensibly to talk fly fishing, there was an underlying desire to enlist people to protect central Pennsylvania's limestone spring creeks. At the time, Fox and Marinaro were deeply involved in the experiments, out of which their books grew, and were among the few people aware of the value of the region's waters. In the Letort, Big Springs, and the Yellow Breeches, they saw waters capable of providing Pennsylvania anglers with fishing equal to that found on England's famous chalk streams. In the club they imagined they would find a means to preserve the streams and educate people of their importance.

The club's first meeting was in 1947 in the Harrisburger Hotel. Meetings were at first conducted once a week. To encourage attendance, and to appease the hotel's management, three types of memberships were established—eating, non-eating, and honorary. Since even a group as loose as the Harrisburg Fly Fishers still needs to correspond and pay postage, a modest assessment was periodically levied on the members. A set of membership rules also were adopted, but these were dropped when the club outgrew its luncheon format.

Luncheon programs of the Harrisburg club revolved around papers written by members and included presentations by some of the best-known names in American fly fishing. The first paper was a humorous look at "Those Pennsylvania Boys" by Sparse Grey Hackle, better known as Alfred Miller, a reporter for the *Wall Street Journal* and the author of *Fishless Days, Angling Nights*. Hackle correctly predicted that Pennsylvania's limestone anglers would influence fly fishing practices throughout America.

The current practice of an annual meeting started at the West Shore Country Club on February 6, 1948, when the guest speaker was another legendary angling figure, Edward R. Hewitt, author of *A Trout and Salmon Fisherman for Seventy-Five Years*. His talk focused on work he was then doing with a refracting tank he had built to try and understand how a trout views flies and leaders. At this meeting, George Harvey, developer of the nation's first accredited college course in fly fishing (at Penn State University in the 1930s), caused a stir when he disputed Hewitt's contention that fine tippets are crucial to successful dry fly fishing. Harvey maintained that leaders designed to delay the onset of drag were more important to dry fly success than tippet size. The elderly and aristocratic Hewitt countered by proclaiming: "Young man, when you are as old as I am, you will realize you were wrong!"

Considering the club's lack of officers and organization, it was inevitable, and unfortunate, that record keeping would suffer. There are no minutes of club meetings after 1948, but the influence of the club and its members has continued. Slaymaker writes:

> The most important contribution of the Fly Fishers Club of Harrisburg was fostering the growth of fly fishing as a conservation-oriented pastime. . . . While many espoused the cause of improved public trout fisheries, there was little incentive on their part for activism. HFF's leaders, to the contrary, took stands and in a real sense led a small band of fly-rod vigilantes whose ranks were open to *all* fly fishermen.

The Cumberland Valley chapter of Trout Unlimited, the first Trout Unlimited chapter in Pennsylvania and the second in the nation, was founded, with Fox as president, during the 1962 banquet. The Harrisburg idea moved west to Pittsburgh with Bob Runk, a native of the Harrisburg area who had learned fly fishing from Fox. Runk moved to Pittsburgh to work for the Westinghouse Electric Corporation in the late 1930s. After attending meetings of the Fly Fishers Club of Harrisburg, in the early 1950s he proposed starting a similar club to a group of engineers at Westinghouse who were interested in fishing. The tradition was passed on as Fox and Marinaro had hoped.

My invitation to the Fly Fishers Club of Harrisburg annual dinner announces Bob Butler as the speaker. I normally pay little attention to such things and the name means nothing to me— until a small gray-haired gentleman steps to the front of the room and I recognize him as the former host of the Public Television series *Outdoor Pennsylvania*. Before entering the world of tele-

George says the drum was more avidly sought by Native Americans living along the Allegheny, Monongahela, and Ohio Rivers, because of the large numbers in which it occurred and its size. Remains have been uncovered of drum weighing up to fifty pounds. In the Susquehanna River the chief catch was shad, and on the Delaware River shad and herring.

Since the Indians fished to obtain food, they naturally sought to catch as many fish as possible at one time, which made the weir their preferred method of fishing. Known as far back as 1000 B.C. the weir is an obvious fishing technology still used by subsistence fishermen in some parts of the world today. The Indians would construct a long triangular-shaped rock dam with an opening at the apex where they would place a woven basket. Then they would get in the river below and drive the fish upstream toward the baskets. Most early weirs on Pennsylvania's major rivers were lost when those rivers were channelized and dammed during the nineteenth century, according to George. However, some weir sites have been reported along smaller streams around the state and may still exist on the upper Youghiogheny River.

Sinker stones and pieces of fabric uncovered by archaeologists show that nets were another fishing method employed by Native Americans. "How far back that technology goes we don't know," George says, "but I am sure it goes back a lot farther than we would like to believe. It's interesting, though," he adds, "that on Monongahela sites net artifacts do not occur, but when you get into northern Pennsylvania on sites from the same time period they do occur. So, the Monongahela were not using that method, but some of the other ones were."

Early Indians also fished individually, with bow and arrow and with hooks and line. Projectile points with an extension on one end have been found and appear to have been made specifically for fishing. The extension may have served as a barb to better hold fish. "It seems logical," George notes, "especially if you are after fish with soft flesh. Drum and catfish are pretty soft. There are no scales on catfish, so you would almost need a point with a barb to pull it out of the water after you shot it."

The Indians carved their hooks out of bone. They were barbless, similar in design to modern hooks—"extremely well made," according to George. Preservation problems have prevented researchers from making a guess as to how far back into pre-Columbian Pennsylvania hooks were used, but what seems logical is that, sometime between five hundred and one thousand years ago, imaginative anglers from various tribes took fur and feathers, tied them to the shank of a hook, and thus became the state's first fly fishermen and fisherwomen.

Although the Indians left no written accounts of their angling exploits, the letters and diaries of early European travelers gush with the angling bounty and pleasures to be found. Thomas Hariot gives the earliest known description of Indians fishing for pleasure with reed rods in *A briefe and true report of the new found land of Virginia*, published in London in 1588. He wrote: "Doubtless yt is a pleasant sighte to see the people, sometymes wadinge and not deepe, free from all care of heaping opp Riches for their posterite, content with their state, and liuing frendlye together of those things which god of his bountye hath giuen vnto them." A 1680 account left by Mahlon Stacy, an early New Jersey settler, describes herring in the Delaware River:

> We drove thousands before us, but so many got into our trap as it would hold. And then we began to haul them on shore, as fast as three or four of us could, but two or three at a time, and after this manner, in a half hour, we could have filled a three bushel sack of as good, large herring as ever I saw. . . . And though I speak of herrings only, lest any should think we have little of other sorts, we have great plenty of most sorts of fish that I ever saw in England, besides several other sorts that are not known there, as rocks, catfish, shads, sheepsheads, sturgeons. . . . Indeed the country, though seen as a wilderness, is a brave country.

A glimpse of the Indians' attitude toward the fish they found around them is given by Francis Parkman, in *The Jesuits in North America in the Seventeenth Century*. The description reveals a respect for their quarry that modern anglers would do well to emulate, at least in spirit:

> To propitiate their fishing-nets, and persuade them to do their office with effect, [they] married them every year to two young girls of the tribe, with a ceremony far more formal than that observed in the case of mere human

wedlock. The fish, too, no less than the nets, must be propitiated; and to this end they were addressed every evening from the fishing-camp by one of the party chosen for that function, who exhorted them to take courage and be caught, assuring them that the utmost respect should be shown to their bones. The harangue, which took place after the evening meal, was made in solemn form; and while it lasted, the whole party, except the speaker, were required to lie on their backs, silent and motionless, around the fire.

William Penn himself was drawn on several occasions to re-mark on the abundance of fish to be found in Pennsylvania wa-ters. In a letter to the Duke of York in January 1683, he wrote: "Our rivers have also plenty of excellent fish and waterfowl, as sturgeon, rock, shad, herring, cod fish, flat-heads, roach and perch and trout in inland streams." Six months later, he noted in a let-ter to the Free Trade Society in London: "Of Fish, there is the Sturgeon, Herring, Rock, Shad, Catshead, Sheepshead, Ele, Smelt, Pearch, Roach; and Inland Rivers, Trout, some say Salmon, above the Falls [of the Delaware River] . . . the Waters are generally good, for the Rivers and Brooks have mostly Gravel and Stony Bottoms, and in Number hardly credible." In the same letter, however, Penn also saw the seeds of the destruction that would destroy Pennsylvania's original fish and wildlife populations. "Since the Europeans came into these parts," Penn wrote, "they [the Indians] are grown great lovers of strong Liquors, Rum espe-cially, and for it exchange the richest of their Skins and Furs."

I can't imagine how ignorant a person must be to dump an easy chair in such a place. Normally, I pick up any trash I find in the woods, but an easy chair is not a can or a bottle. There is little I can do about it, alone and without a truck. Angry, but resigned, I turn away from the stream and pull out my wading bag.

Once dressed, I notice a path leading upstream. At first I am disappointed to see the opening in the brush, but an absence of footprints and the vagueness of its outline indicate it has not been used much. I guess that it also gets fainter the farther upstream it goes since few fishermen like to walk to their fishing. About twenty yards into the woods, I spot a trout lily growing along the path. When I was younger and catching fish was the only thing on my mind, I would have passed the flower by with barely a glance, but as I have grown older, such sights have become more important to me. I've even been trying to learn the names of wild flowers. Now I take pride in being able to identify trout lilies, trilliums, buttercups, bluebells, mayflowers, coltsfoots, dame's rockets, daylilies, yellow violets, jack-in-the-pulpits, and wild geraniums. It's not much, but it's a start.

A few yards beyond the trout lily the stream bends and forms a small pool. I tie on an Adams and start to cast, but there's a downed tree along the bank that gets in the way. The fly lands awkwardly on the clear water. The wake of a fleeing trout cuts the surface. I do not have the patience at the moment for such tight fishing. After a few more tries, I give up and move on to explore the stream for other days. From the bend I continue upstream, mentally marking pools and holes where trout might hide. I find several places I would like to try later in the season when my casting is sharper and when leaves cover the surface in shadow. Right now, the sun coming through the bare trees is so bright I can count the pebbles on the bottom. I decide to head for Laurel Hill Creek.

The Laurel Highlands generally are not thought of as prime trout country. More than a century of supplying the steel mills of Pittsburgh with coal has destroyed many of their rivers and streams, but the region also contains many spots where nature has recovered from the laissez-faire attitude of the Industrial Revolution. In places, the land has returned to something approximating what George Washington saw in 1754 when he ignited the French and Indian War at Fort Necessity on Laurel Hill.

Nobody of my acquaintance knows more about trout fishing in the Laurel Highlands than Tim McKula. He has fished the waters surrounding Laurel Hill for more than thirty-five years and has a family history of fishing the region that goes back to World War I. For more than a quarter-century, Tim has made his home on Chestnut Ridge and for almost as long has been keeping tabs on the region's trout waters. Both on his own and as a volunteer for the Alliance for Acid Rain Monitoring, Tim has tested the water quality of most streams within a twenty-mile radius of his home, using a pH meter and titration device to test alkalinity. He has found that a pH of 6.5 and higher, combined with an alkalinity reading of 30 or more parts per million, is a direct reflection of a stream's health.

"That's not to say streams without free alkalinity and a poor pH don't have fish, because they do," he says.

A lot of native brook trout streams will carry hardly any free alkalinity and I've seen them with pHs of less than six-five, even into the high fives, and have pretty good populations. But they're sterile streams and the fish are not big. Where there are native brook trout streams in this area that carry good alkaline water, wild brown trout have taken them over. . . . There are fishermen who complain that we are losing our native brook trout, but I kind of like it to be honest because brown trout are harder to catch. I don't know what the reason may be, but very few of those fish get caught by bait fishermen. The guys who get them are fly fishermen. Most fishermen in the area go in and take the stocked fish out and as soon as those are gone they leave. From mid-May on, the area is wide open to fly fishermen and there aren't any fly fishermen fishing most of the systems up here. So, those guys who do fly fish have the Laurel Highlands practically to themselves.

The only major eastern mayfly species Tim has never found in the Laurel Highlands is the Brown Drake. Most seasons he finds hatches of Quill Gordons, Sulphurs, Hendericksons, Green Drakes, March Browns, Grey Fox, Light Cahills, Blue-Winged Olives, and even Tricos, which are more associated with limestone streams. "We get some spectacular Green Drakes hatches on small streams," he adds. "But a lot of the Green Drake hatches are short-lived. I've seen them on the water as long as five days and as short as three days. So you have to keep checking."

As I near Laurel Hill State Park, a raven and then two deer appear on the road. The deer are big and fat, which leads me to infer that winter on the mountain has been easy and deer season will be good. The Pittsburgh radio station I'm listening to flutters and fades and is replaced by a twangy-accented woman's voice warning of eternal damnation. When fire and brimstone replaces rock 'n' roll on the radio, I know I'm in Pennsylvania trout country.

Laurel Hill Creek is a deep green and there is only one vehicle parked along the dirt road that runs through its Delayed Harvest Project. This makes me think maybe I've made a bad choice, for when fishing is good the road is usually lined with vehicles. Then I see that the large rocks near the center of the project are submerged. The water is not only higher than I expected but higher than I can recall ever seeing. Since I've made the drive and haven't fished for a couple of weeks, though, I pull over.

For half an hour, I beat the water with everything I can think of. I fish the bottom, the mid-depths, and the surface, fast water and eddies, the edges of runs, tight against the rocks and logs, in the shallows along the banks. I try black and brown stoneflies, Hare's Ears, Pheasant Tails, Olive and Orange Soft-Hackles, black and chartreuse Wooly Buggers, Green and Strawberry Weenies, Glo Bugs, Adams, Humphies, Royal Wulffs, Elk Hair Caddis, and even a big Irish Mayfly without moving a single fish. Disappointed, I think of heading to Jones Mill Run, a tributary of Laurel Hill in the park, but I am just not in the mood for such small water. Then I remember another stream, between Laurel Hill and Jones Mill in size, that might be a compromise. Tim claims it is one of the most fertile streams in the Laurel Highlands. He has found all the major eastern hatches on it.

Off the road leading past Seven Springs Resort, the woods are packed with snow. Blocks large enough for snowmen line the berm of the road. Runoff from the melting snow is the reason Laurel Hill Creek is so high, I think. I vaguely recall a weather report on Sunday predicting three inches of snow in the mountains.

Parked next to the bridge when I arrive at the stream is an

enormous old Buick, more rust and primer than paint. As I near the beast a sinewy man with dark hair combed in a DA emerges from the rhododendron. Tattoos cover his arms. There is a pack of cigarettes rolled up in the sleeve of his white T-shirt and he is carrying a heavy, worm-baited spinning outfit. Hurriedly, he walks over to the bridge, peers down into the water on both sides, then throws the rod into the back seat of the Buick and takes off in a plume of loose gravel. For a moment I wonder if I've crossed some sort of Twilight Zone back into the 1950s.

Once the Buick is gone, I step over to the bridge and check out the stream. Like Laurel Hill Creek, it is running high. But its water is clear and looks as if it might produce a fish or two. I take out my rod and walk about a hundred yards up the road, then cut through an opening in the rhododendron.

No sooner do I reach the water than I spot four or five mayflies dancing overhead. I think they are Quill Gordons, but before I can decide, my attention is distracted by a smell of decay and I look down to find myself standing in a garbage dump next to a dead deer. Shaking my head in disgust at the dump, too common of a sight along Pennsylvania's back roads, I back out of the rhododendron and return to the bridge where I drop my Green Weenie into the first pool and immediately hook a small brookie. The catch is my first of the open season, but my heart is no longer into fishing.

tory and Biography, Davis Hugh Davis, a Quaker who kept the George Inn from 1773 to 1778, "was famous for making fishing tackle, deep-seas, fly feather etc. His operation for fastening the hooks & other light work was carried on during school hours, 8 till 12 & 2 to 5, after taking his rounds."

Since the first American sporting periodical did not appear until 1829, and no American wrote a fishing book until 1845, evidence of Philadelphia as the hotbed of sport fishing activity is largely circumstantial. There were certainly gentlemen and gentlewomen in other locations who also were fishing for amusement. No movement as massive and diverse as angling could have developed in any one single area. Advances in technology are too dependent on individuals, and it is not unusual for two, three, or a dozen anglers to reach the same conclusions about tackle and techniques, independently, without any knowledge of each other—and to leave no record. Nevertheless, the presence of clubs such as the Schuylkill Fishing Company, the success of Edward Pole, George Lawton, and their fellow tackle dealers, and the renown of fly tier Davis Hugh Davis, all point to a deep interest in sport fishing among early citizens of the City of Brotherly Love that went well beyond mere subsistence.

Mandrake Magic

The day after my trip to Laurel Hill it starts to rain again. When it finally stops, three days later, I find myself trapped in the making of a living, and forced to take comfort in thoughts of the streams being muddy and unfishable. Then, when work finally permits a day off, it rains again. Once more, two full weeks pass before the weather and my life come into sync again, and I can return to Laurel Hill. I hope a pattern isn't forming.

Scenery occasionally plays a more important role in my selection of a fishing spot than the chance of fish. Sometimes I simply want to be in a quiet place where the mountains drop down to the water and hemlocks make everything dark and cool. So, when I reach the center of Laurel Hill's Delayed Harvest Project, I head downstream to its fast water and its tangled mountain laurel, and away from the flats I love so much. The greatest fun in fishing for me is in seeing the take, and no place is better for that than the flats. Finding a trout rising on the flats, understanding what it is feeding on, choosing the right fly, timing the rise, laying out a perfect cast, then watching the fish drift up from the bottom to take, this is the top of the angling food chain as far as I am concerned. It isn't sport. It's art. A play. "The Catch."

Since the water in the lower half of the project is fast, all I see when I cast my orange soft-hackle toward the log lying along the far bank is a flash of silver. Then I feel a weight and see a head shaking hard side to side. Caught off guard by the ferocity of the strike and the bulk of the fish, I react without thinking, raising my rod tip high—instead of dropping it low in a way that would put side pressure on the fish and coax it away from the log. To feel himself being lifted from his watery world makes the trout fight harder, and within a few seconds leaves me reeling in my fly and swearing at my stupidity. As if force of will might bring him back, I cast at the log again and again until I finally have to admit the trout is gone.

I am wondering what to do next when two fish rise in the riffle above the log and my mind is made up for me. Hurriedly, I exchange the soft-hackle for an Adams and drop a cast above the first fish. When nothing happens, I try another cast, and then another and another, until it becomes clear that neither fish has the slightest interest. I give up the Adams for an Elk Hair Caddis. When this fails, I switch to a red ant, then a black ant, and a Renegade. Soon I am rummaging through my boxes pulling out beetles and inchworms, Hendricksons, Blue-Winged Olives, and Quill Gordons. Nothing works. When I check my watch, I see forty-five minutes have passed. It is almost five-thirty. I think the fish might be on midges, but when I look into the box that contains those tiny flies, I don't feel up to the challenge. I close the lid and move on.

Like many of my friends, I have mixed feelings about special regulation waters such as Laurel Hill Creek's Delayed Harvest Project. I dislike them because they attract crowds; I like them because they allow me to fish year-round over a large number of trout. Although there have been streams in Pennsylvania with special regulations since at least the early nineteenth century, the laws governing them were either passed by local municipalities or enacted by individuals or clubs that controlled the water. The beginning of public special regulation projects goes back only to the Great Depression and to Fisherman's Paradise.

Located on Spring Creek, Centre County, Fisherman's Paradise was originally developed as a showcase remedy to a continuous loss of public fishing waters. By the start of the 1930s, approximately three-quarters of the mileage of Pennsylvania's major streams was unfishable due to acid mine drainage, industrial and municipal pollution. Of the remaining trout water, about one mile in seven was leased by clubs or individuals and closed to fishing, while one-fourth of what had formerly been open was posted by landowners angry about littering and other such disrespectful angler behavior. Compounding these problems was a five-year-long drought, which drew predators to the few remaining pools, where they feasted royally on the trapped fish.

To determine what remained of suitable trout water, the Fish Commission in 1931 launched a four-year survey of all Pennsylvania's rivers, lakes, and streams. The survey was the first comprehensive look at the state's waterways ever to be conducted, and it found that for each mile of stream capable of supporting fish, there were approximately four and a half miles of water so polluted that no type of aquatic life could exist in it. The survey also revealed "the astounding fact that should our anglers all go astream on the same day, available fishing waters would be so congested that each fisherman would have available only ninety feet of stream as his territory."

Hoping to "make two blades of grass grow where one grew before," the Fish Commission turned for suggestions to Edward R. Hewitt and the stream improvement work he had done on New York's Neversink River. The commission decided to build a model project in the center of the state, where anglers could visit and take home ideas on how to improve the streams where they lived. At the same time, a section of Spring Creek became available for sale and was purchased by the Fish Commission. To encourage anglers to visit the project, the commission decided to offer "trout fishing de luxe." Some 9,000 trout were stocked in the project's mile and a quarter of stream. On opening day in 1934, for the first season of Fisherman's Paradise, approximately 3,000 people visited the project, including 472 anglers who registered to fish, as was required at the time. A total of 4,808 would register that first season and 6,163 during its second season in 1935.

Along with stream improvement, Fisherman's Paradise sought to promote a very new idea as well, that of catch-and-release. Anglers that first season were permitted to catch and release fifteen trout per day (then the limit in Pennsylvania), but to kill only two fish of ten inches or larger. All fishing was limited to artificial lures with barbless hooks. Such regulations caused some members of the Fish Commission to worry about an angry response from anglers accustomed to killing practically every trout they caught. Once again the public was ahead of the government, though. Oliver Deibler, then director of the commission, wrote: "Many expert anglers refused to kill any. One particular chap told me on the closing day of the season last year that he could not afford to kill fish so valuable to the sportsman. He felt the same was true of other sportsmen—that they [the fish] were worth many times more alive in the stream where they could furnish sport—than they were dead in his creel."

Reasoning that "when we succeed in selling fishing to our wives and sweethearts in a thorough manner, it will not be necessary in the future for us men folks to manufacture so many excuses and unbelievable stories as has been the rule when we were contemplating a fishing trip," the commission set aside a quarter-mile stretch of the project for ladies only. To aid the ladies, many of whom had never fished before, the commission also supplied an instructor to teach them how to cast a fly. The result was that 266 lady anglers fished the project during its first season, and 647 in its second year, an increase of about 300 percent!

As a direct result of Fisherman's Paradise, stream improvement projects were begun in seventeen counties by members of sportsmen's groups who had visited the project during its first year. Financed with half a million dollars from the Works Progress Administration, this total grew to include projects in fifty counties by the second year, making Fisherman's Paradise a milestone in fisheries management.

Above the Chapel Hole, named for the tiny, nondenominational chapel that stands above it, I run into an old fisherman whom I have seen along the stream in the past. Even before we exchange greetings, he is telling me about the caddis hatch he ran into upstream and the twenty-seven trout he caught. He says the hatch is over—but I expect nothing better and decide to head to the stretch thinking I might catch a few stragglers. My hopes appear answered when I reach the pool and spot two fish dimpling the surface in the shadow of current coming off a submerged rock. One is at the top of the current, the other at the tail. They are far enough apart that I think I can take both of them if I am careful.

Sliding down the bank I spook two more fish. Fortunately, they make their escape downstream away from the risers and I am able to work my way into casting position under a large oak. Some anglers laugh at wearing chest waders in small streams, but as I kneel in the mud I realize once more—chest waders are a good way to keep a dry ass. Keeping low pays off. Within a few minutes I hook, land, and release both fish. Then I spot several others rising sporadically and quickly push my total up to six, my biggest catch of the season so far. When no more risers appear, I decide to explore. As many times as I've fished Laurel Hill, I cannot recall ever having been so far upstream. I have to pause as I enter the woods. Spread everywhere around me is the most intense plain of mayapples I've ever seen. They cover the forest floor like umbrellas during a rainy Steelers' game, reminding me of Alice in Wonderland.

Also known as the American mandrake, the original mayapple of Europe was the most revered of all medicinal herbs. During medieval times, mandrake roots carved to resemble tiny human figures were sold all over Europe for use in medicine and magic (not necessarily two separate pursuits in those days). When early European settlers learned from the Indians that the mayapple was valuable as a medicine, they transferred the name *mandrake* and much of the Old World plant's traditional lore to the mayapple, even though the two plants are unrelated. According to *Edible Wild Plants of Pennsylvania and Neighboring States* by Richard and Mary Lee Medve, the mayapple-derived compound peltatine is used today in cancer research. But what I find most fascinating is that the huge colony spread before me has sprung from one single, interconnected root system—the little umbrellas are not individual plants.

On the other side of the mayapple patch, Laurel Hill turns nearly stagnant. I find a pair of Canada geese drifting on it. The geese quietly float off when I enter the water and cross to the opposite bank. Then I spot a rise on the next bend. Slowly, I move closer and begin to work out line. My first few casts are off the mark. Then I hook a dead branch hanging over the water. Hoping to save my fly, I point my rod tip at the snag and gently pull on the line. A fly often can be freed by pointing the rod tip at the snag and slowly drawing the line tight, then releasing it. This time, though, the branch is so rotten that, when the line tightens, it breaks off and falls almost on top of the trout. Hoping to avoid disturbing the pool anymore, I wait for the branch to drift down to me, then untangle my fly and think I've at least saved some other fisherman from a similar fate.

With the fish on the bend gone, I wonder what to do next. Then I catch a glimpse of a ring disappearing in the whisper of current coming off a rock below me. I drop a cast ahead of the current, watch as the fly drifts closer and the fish rises, following, following, following, until I'm sure he is going to turn away. Then he fools me, strikes, and is gone.

"You bastard!" I shout, not so much in anger, but in respect for an opponent who has beaten me. Then I notice the trout on the bend has returned. I cast toward his ring and on the third try miss him, too. He continues to feed, and I wait a minute to make sure he is into a rhythm, then try once more. When he ignores my Elk Hair Caddis, I think maybe I should try something different and strip in line to find that the hook is broken. The point must have snapped when I hooked the dead branch. I feel stupid for not having checked it, but at the same time happy it was not my timing that caused me to miss. I tie on an Adams and try for the fish on the bend until I put him down again, and I give up on the pool.

Back at the oak tree, I find two fish again rising in the riffle. On the second cast, I take the one on the far edge. It is a rainbow of about eleven inches, my first rainbow of the season. Then, a minute later, I have the second fish, and in rapid succession a third, a fourth, and a fifth. The action does not stop until I've hooked seven, giving me a total of thirteen for the day. It is my highest total of the season so far. I feel contented.

Of Sounds, Memories, and Trophies

One good day promising another, I am back on Laurel Hill Creek the following afternoon. I am there even though experience long ago taught me the opposite is more often true on the stream and my chances of catching another hatch and rising trout are about as good as hitting the daily number. Fishing is faith, however, and my hopes rise when the first person I encounter is the old gentleman who told me about the caddis hatch. This time he is not fishing. He is patrolling the Delayed Harvest Project for people who are using bait or keeping fish, which is prohibited until June 15, more than a month away.

"I caught two kids with fish last week," he says proudly. "One had five, the other seven. Caught a guy with bait, too. I turned them all in."

"It's a shame," I answer, a standard refrain in such conversations. "It only takes a couple of people to ruin it for everybody."

"Well, they're not gonna get away with it with me," he adds. Then he asks how I did yesterday. Before I can answer, he checks his watch, tells me his wife is waiting in the car, and he's gone, leaving me full of admiration.

When a squadron of caddis flies flutter past my head, I look down at the Chapel Hole to find trout midging, but I am not interested. I've fished the hole too many times over the years. I want something new.

Creek, something I found to be true when five fish fell to it on my first try.

This time, nothing happens, however. The fish continue to rise, showing no interest whatsoever in the Cooper Bug. Something smaller is needed, but I don't like to go too small. I drop down one hook size to a No. 16 red ant, and that's enough. Quickly, I miss three fish, then a fourth, which comes out of nowhere and smashes the ant so hard I am left cursing and openmouthed with a tangled leader. Encouraged by the possibility, I spend the next twenty minutes fishing the pool with everything I can think of, until I finally come to the conclusion that it is probably just going to be one of those days.

On the flats below the Chapel Hole, I notice for the first time the heat and humidity of the evening. Sweat runs down my sides, reminding me of the sweltering, haze-filled afternoons on the limestone streams of the Cumberland Valley—the Letort, the Yellow Breeches, Falling Spring—when it was so bad, on occasion, that I was courting heatstroke and had to dunk my hat in the chilly waters of those spring creeks to cool my head. It was always worth it, though, for the chance to fool trout during the dog days of August.

The writings of Vince Marinaro, Charlie Fox, and a dozen others have made these limestone streams the most famous trout waters in Pennsylvania. The first time I heard about them was more than twenty years ago, when I wandered into the fly shop Bill Lang ran out of his garage in the small Westmoreland County town of Penn. I was learning how to tie flies at the time, and Bill's shop was the only place in the area to buy materials. That afternoon he was full of excitement over the weekend he had just spent fishing the trico hatch on Falling Spring.

"It was absolutely incredible," he told me in that quiet way he had even when excited. "The fish were going wild. You'd be casting to one and a breeze would come up and blow your fly aside and another one would take it."

I had no idea what a trico might be, but I wanted such fishing. I asked Bill to tie me a dozen of the flies, took down directions on how to reach the stream, and then talked John Stephens, one of the part-time employees in the sporting goods store I managed, into going to Chambersburg with me.

When I picked up the flies the Thursday before our trip, I nearly went into shock. I had never seen a No. 26 hook before, never even knew such a thing existed. The sporting goods store I ran was part of a chain with a clientele that ran more toward hunting, spin fishing, softball, and camping. I couldn't imagine a fish taking such a tiny fly, no bigger than a flea it seemed, or that I had paid six dollars for the specks of black-and-white thread in my hand.

When I showed the flies to John, he could only say: "You're kidding!"

Those were the same words he used when we first laid eyes on Falling Spring. We were accustomed to the tumbling, laurel-lined streams of Pennsylvania's mountains, and Falling Spring looked to our eyes like a ditch draining a pasture.

"Trout live in that?" John asked incredulously. Neither of us caught a fish that first trip, but we saw plenty and they were rising steadily. That was enough to bring me back the following weekend, when I did catch three.

Over the next decade, I managed to make five or six trips a summer to the limestone streams, settling into a pattern that revolved around the morning spinner fall of tricos on Falling Spring, followed by the afternoon and evening on the Yellow Breeches. Occasionally, there were side trips to Green Spring and Big Spring, which was a total disappointment, the most beautiful of all Pennsylvania's limestone streams ruined by a polluting hatchery at its source. Then there was the stream that scared me—the Letort.

I shunned the Letort because Marinaro's *A Modern Dry-Fly Code* had become my favorite angling book, and it made the stream nearly mythical in my mind. I could not imagine measuring up to a water as demanding as the one described in that book. The awed talk of the Letort I encountered on the Yellow Breeches and Falling Spring only added to the myth.

"Have you been to the Letort yet?" someone would ask, and then shake his head and let out a silent whistle. The first couple of times I visited the stream, I didn't dare wet a line.

Then, alone one afternoon, I took a ride to Fox's Meadow and found a trout rising regularly next to a clump of sod protected by an overhanging choke cherry tree and screen of blackberry bushes and wild roses. Recalling the chumming Marinaro and Fox sometimes did with Japanese beetles, I collected a small handful of the coppery insects from the rose bushes and dropped them one at a time into the current on which the fish was feeding. As in their books, the trout rose to take the beetles, one after the other. The stage was set.

Tossing my last two beetles into the water, I carefully made my way around the blackberry and rose screen and slipped into the water. Knowing that everything would have to be absolutely perfect if I was ever to fool a Letort trout, I waited until the water was flowing quietly again and the fish rose once, twice, three times, making it clear he had no idea I existed. Then I tied on one of the Jassids I'd made especially for the occasion—a fly invented by Marinaro, which Ernest Schwiebert once used to catch fifty Letort trout, or some equally incredible number—and began to work out line.

My first cast fell about fifteen inches to the right and made me think I had blown it, but as I waited for the line to drift down to me the fish rose again and soothed my fears. Then, as the line floated nearer, my right foot began to sink into the muck of the bottom until it felt as if I was going to tumble head first into the creek. Hoping to at least keep free of the line that was starting to wrap around me, I flicked my rod and sent a cast upstream at the same moment I lunged for the bank. Splashing and grabbing at the grass of the bank, I knew my chance for the fish was gone, and then I lifted my rod to feel its weight on the other end.

From the rocks that border the flats, I watch the surface for several minutes without detecting a rise. It is beginning to feel as if it is time to move on, when a wake shows alongside the downed tree that lies across the Chapel Hole and what looks like the tail of a mallard pokes out of the water. I feel proud and excited that I can be so unobtrusive a duck will bury its head to feed near me. But when the tail doesn't move or the head appear after what seems too long a time, I wonder what is going on. My question is answered when the creature crawls out of the water onto the log. It is a beaver.

Twice now I've encountered beavers on Laurel Hill Creek. For several years a gnawed birch trunk below Laurel Hill Lake told me beaver were on the stream, but it was not until last year that I actually saw one. It was a quiet May evening. Limbs stripped clean of bark and lying bright on the bottom said beavers were nearby, but I never expected to see one. My concentration was focused on the fish along the opposite bank. I never noticed the beaver when it surfaced a few yards below me, and because I was obscured by a branch, he didn't see me until I took a step into the pool. He slapped his tail so loud and so close, I literally jumped and, propelled by a shot of adrenaline, backed out of the water ready to flee or fight.

I watch the beaver until it slips off the log and vanishes under the surface. Then a set of rise rings appear under a bush growing out of the opposite bank. I send a cast toward the rings. The trout rises. Either it changes its mind and turns or I strike too quickly and miss the opportunity. Before I can decide what went wrong, a second fish provides me with a chance for redemption when it breaks water in the riffle feeding the pool. Once again I am caught off guard when it hits the instant the fly touches the water.

"Damn!" I swear at myself.

For the next half hour, I match wits with the two trout until a stiffness in my back forces me to turn away. As I look off into the woods, my eyes react as if they are viewing the world through a veil. I've been staring at the surface of the stream for so long everything is distorted. I squint and blink in an attempt to change the focus of my eyes. Then, looking back at the stream, I notice that the surface is covered with tiny rings. Mayflies, I think, until I feel rain. A moment later the sky splits open and sends me hurrying for my car.

G.

The first Gibsons are believed to have arrived in the Delaware Valley from Scotland in 1674. George the elder moved from Philadelphia to Lancaster County in 1720, where he operated the Hickory Tree Tavern, around which the city of Lancaster was laid out ten years later. Again giving in to the lure of western lands, the family moved from Lancaster to the Cumberland Valley in 1770, where George the elder's son, George senior, became owner of a mill on Silver Spring near Carlisle. Two years later, George senior married Anne West, a cousin of the famed colonial portrait painter Benjamin West. In 1773 George senior and Anne moved from Silver Spring over Blue Mountain to property Anne's father owned on Sherman Creek at Westover Mills, Perry County. It was there that George Patrick Henry Gibson—one of the nation's first angling writers and the man who introduced the world to sport fishing in Pennsylvania—was born, most likely on September 11, 1775.

Like countless boys, before and since, Gibson was instilled early on with a love of the outdoors by his father. George senior was a restless man who craved adventure and was always riding off to fish and hunt. "Fox hunting, fishing, gunning, rifle shooting, swimming, wrestling and boxing with the natives of my age, were my exercises and my amusement," Gibson's brother John writes. Celebrated as a humorist and a wit, George senior also would seem to have been the source for his son's storytelling abilities and congenial style.

George senior's craving for action led him to join General Arthur St. Clair's 1791 expedition against British-supported Indians raiding settlements in the Ohio Valley. He marched with St. Clair to Fort Washington in Cincinnati, and then west to the Wabash River, where the fourteen-hundred-man army was caught by surprise on the morning of November 4, 1791. When the smoke cleared, more than six hundred officers and men were either dead or missing, and nearly three hundred others wounded. It was the worst defeat the U.S. Army would ever suffer at the hands of the Indians. Wounded in the head early in the engagement, George senior fought on until struck in the body by a second ball, and then in the wrist by a third. Carried to Fort Jefferson about sixty miles north of Fort Washington, he died a few days later.

Left with only a mill and seventy-eight acres of mountainous land, Anne Gibson was nevertheless determined that her children would have an education. She built a school near the family home and taught the children herself. She did such a good job that Gibson was hired as an accountant by a Baltimore importer when he was twenty years old. She was also a devout Episcopalian, who every Sunday made the fifteen-mile trip from her home to St. Johns Church in Carlisle. Anne wanted her children baptized. One day she prevailed upon a visiting minister to accompany her home for that purpose, which resulted in an amusing, if unintentional, collision of religion, boys, and outdoors.

"It so happened that all four of the boys were off on a hunt that day in the mountains," writes Thomas Roberts in *Memoirs of John Bannister Gibson*, George's younger brother who became a chief justice of the Pennsylvania Supreme Court,

> and as they did not return until late, the household, with
> its distinguished visitor, was sound asleep before they came
> in; the baptism was necessarily postponed until the mor-
> row. The boys knew nothing of this arrangement, and as
> game tracked best in the early morning, they started before
> day-break to conclude the chase abandoned the evening
> before. Just how the old lady explained matters to the
> bishop at "coffee and muffins" that morning, and the boys
> absence from the table, is not told, but it is very easy to

imagine that as he rode away without having performed his duty, he believed that Perry county required more wide-awake missionaries than the church usually sends to the heathen in other lands.

As he had inherited his father's love of the outdoors and his storytelling abilities, so did Gibson follow George senior's lead into the military. He entered the army as a captain in May 1808 with a troop he partly recruited in Lancaster, and he served during the War of 1812. Discharged in June 1815, he remained a civilian less than a year before reenlisting. Gibson was assigned to the Southern Division of the army under General Andrew Jackson, who was then engaged in fighting the Seminoles in Florida. "He felt that the soldiers of that army were his children, and he provided as the father of a family for their necessities," writes S. Horace Porter, an attorney and friend of Gibson's from Lancaster. "The slightest complaint of the quality of their rations met at once an examination, and if found just, was soon remedied."

The concern Gibson showed for the troops and the way he discharged his duties caught the eye of the general, and the two men became friends. Jackson mentions Gibson in a number of letters, several times as a friend of Mrs. Jackson. "I should do violence to my feelings if I did not particularly notice the exertions of my Qr Master General Col George Gibson," he notes in a letter to Secretary of War John C. Calhoun, "who under the most embarrassing of circumstances relieved the necessities of my army and to whose exertions was I indebted for the supplies received. His zeal and integrity on this campaign as well as in the uniform discharge of his duties since his connection with my staff merits the approbation and gratitude of his country."

In April 1818, Gibson was appointed commissary general of the army. It was a position he would hold for the next forty-three years. Along with military matters, references to Gibson and horse racing also appear in Jackson's letters. He seems to have been a well-known horseman of the period. It was probably through his racing and breeding activities that he came to the attention of New Yorker John Skinner and became a correspondent for the *American Turf Register and Sporting Magazine*.

Outdoor magazines in the early nineteenth century were far different from those today. Like the English periodicals upon which they were modeled (and from which they often stole stories), they were heavily devoted to turf activities. Fishing and hunting were peripheral to horsemanship, which is understandable, considering the importance of the horse to daily life in an agrarian society before the invention of the internal combustion engine. For his first story (the first magazine article ever to appear on angling in Pennsylvania and the first of an entire body of literature to spring from the region), Gibson turned to the limestone streams. "Trout Fishing in Cumberland County, Pa." was printed in the premier issue of the *Turf Register* in September 1829. Its focus was Big Spring, the Letort, and Silver Spring, and the tackle and techniques employed to fool their fish.

The article also contains the first plea for the conservation of trout water to appear in an American sporting magazine, an extraordinary example of foresight, considering that the United States was barely half-settled and was looked upon by practically everyone as a land of endless plenty. In the article, Gibson compares the abundance of fish in Big Spring, which was protected by a local law prohibiting netting, to the decline of fish on the unprotected waters of the Letort and Silver Spring. He concludes the story with a humorous description of an evening spent on Silver Spring:

> The proprietor of the grounds advised me to take bait. He had never been successful with a fly. I would not be advised. The evening was fine—a cloud obscured the sun, a gentle breeze rippled the pool, and such was my success, that in less than one hour, I landed twenty trout, from one to two pounds each. The proprietor cried "enough."—I asked for the privilege of another cast. I made one, and hooked a large trout with my bobbing fly, and in playing him, another of equal size ran at and was hooked by my trail fly, and both were landed in handsome style. The last throw was fatal to my sport in that pool—for I never after was a welcome visitor.

Gibson also wrote for the *Spirit of the Times*, an even more influential sporting magazine of the early nineteenth century, which began publishing in 1831. His stories were usually short, written in the form of personal letters. Unlike modern angling writers who crave recognition and scramble to attach their names and faces to merchandise, Gibson and his contemporaries seldom signed their stories, except for initials or pseudonyms such as "Walton," "Piscator," and "Tom Tackle," making identification difficult. Occasionally, the *Turf Register* and the *Spirit of the Times* contain notes on authors, or letters referring to stories in which names are revealed, and certain correspondents signed their stories in certain ways and wrote about particular areas and subjects. Stories signed "G." definitely belonged to Gibson; others signed "M.G.," which focus on Cumberland County, were most likely written by him. There are many others that bear no indication of author, but for style and content might have been written by him.

He considered himself only a "practical man in such matters," but Gibson's correspondence with the *Turf Register* and the *Spirit of the Times* are important for the window they open on angling attitudes, stream conditions, and problems involving fishing in Pennsylvania in the 1830s and 1840s. In "Trout Fishing in the Neighborhood of Carlisle," in the August 1830 issue of the *Turf Register*, Gibson writes of flies and tactics that worked well during a season of heavy rain when the trout turned "very capricious in their feeding." His confusion at failing to take fish, and the way he constantly changed flies in search of success, show him to have been an innovative angler open to experimentation:

At my first visit to Big spring, a dun wing over a red heckle, was a killing fly; but in a few days after, at the same place, not a trout would rise at it; and at Silver spring, a miller sucked in the upper pool, while in that below, a peacock body and brown wind, was the only fly to be relied on. In Letart [Letort], a small grey fly was at all times in season. The trout this year were fat, plump, and of high flavour, but the number taken by a brother sportsman and myself, bears no comparison with that of former years. In our various excursions, we took between seven and eight dozen, and of all sizes, from eight to sixteen inches. I have been particular in noting the colour of my flies and the frequent changes necessary for the benefit of young sportsmen; but they too often stick to the same fly, and the same spot of ground, when they ought to change both.

The same story also profiles "Laughing Jo," an angler whose skills Gibson greatly admired. He uses their encounter along Big Spring to promote sportsmanship, although his measure of sportsmanship is quite a bit different from what we use today:

> "Laughing Jo," adds to his character of a scientific and practical fisherman, that of a modest, sober and hard working man. Jo makes his own lines and flies, holds a rod eighteen feet long, and throws thirty-six or forty feet of line with one hand, and no amateur can avoid a bush, flank an eddy, or drop into a ripple, with more certainty or with more ease. And there is one trait in his character decidedly sportsman—*he never sold a trout in his life;* the produce of his rod is made a grateful offering for favours received.

As was normal for anglers of the period, Gibson fished with wet flies. Being innovative, though, there no doubt were times when he noticed trout rising, dried his wet fly so it would float, and occasionally took a fish on the surface. Austin Hogan, past curator of the American Museum of Fly Fishing, even thought he recognized the forerunners of some modern flies, including the Henderickson, in Gibson's list of patterns. Whether this is true it is impossible to say, however, since his descriptions are so general, usually limited to the color of the body and hackle.

Still, Gibson's choice of flies gives an idea of what patterns and approaches were being used in the state before the Civil War. He writes:

> It is nonsense to believe there is a colour for every month— it is not so—for in fishing three mill pools on the same stream on the same day, I have found that to be successful, I had to change my fly and the colour of it at each pool; and in fishing in the same places a few days after, the only fly trout would rise to, was a small grey one, and to such a one they would rise freely in all the pools. In the early part of the season when the trout is poor, he will run at anything; but towards June he becomes a perfect epicure in his feeding at such time.

Gibson goes on to observe that his "limped lime-stone brooks" require more attention to catch fish on a fly than necessary elsewhere. But, as always, there is the exception and even the most finicky trout sometimes seem bent on suicide:

> I was casting [on Big Spring] a drab fly but did not land
> many fish. In taking my hook from the fourth or fifth trout,
> I discovered that nothing remained of the fly but the
> mohair body, and that somewhat worn. I thought it strange
> that I could take fine fish with such a nondescript fly, so
> unlike any I had ever seen. I tried again, and such was my
> success that Mr. Caruthers left his stand and came up to
> look at my fly. I clipped the wings from one like that on my
> line and gave it to him, and with those two flies we took
> about fifty brace of trout.

Naturally, he reports, the fly never worked again.

Perhaps because he fought them in the War of 1812, Gibson takes a certain joy in ridiculing the stuffy angling habits of the British. One day while on Silver Spring, he overheard someone talking to himself:

> It seemed, by what I could gather from his broken accents,
> that he had been trying some gorgeous flies of *English
> make*: but . . . the fish are so republican in the waters of
> Pennsylvania, that not a trout will strike at foreign bait.
> Our Friend . . . seemed a little mortified at the coarse taste
> that would gorge a fat worm and shy a splendid fly, all the
> way from "London Town."

Between fishing and hunting trips, Gibson fought in the Mexican War. He was promoted to major general in May 1848, and several sources mention him as a close friend of General Winfield Scott, commander of American forces in the Mexican War. Gibson's friendship with Scott may be questionable, however, since his name never appears in Scott's memoirs, but that Gibson was well liked and respected by his fellow officers is beyond doubt. Often they refer to him as being friendly, generous, helpful, and fair, attributes probably enhanced by his days spent fishing.

Gibson never married, but apparently he wanted to since he was president of the Hope Club, an informal group of bachelor officers stationed in Washington, D.C. When he died on September 30, 1861, he was the oldest officer in the U.S. Army and flags were lowered to half-staff and thirteen gun salutes fired at every military base in the nation.

The Great White Fleet

$\mathcal{I}$ get the first hint that I might be in the wrong place at the wrong time when I see six vehicles parked at the old bridge piers. My suspicion grows stronger when another five cars appear at the next pull-off, and then three more a short distance beyond. By the time the dirt road into State Game Lands 51 comes in sight, I have counted more than two dozen cars, trucks, and vans. It is a Monday afternoon, and I am puzzled by the number of people on the water. Then it hits me. Stocking day.

When I was a reporter on a small newspaper, writing a weekly outdoors column, every March I would get a news release from the Fish and Boat Commission proclaiming "Great White Fleet Rolling." The accompanying story would be about the start of the commission's annual trout-stocking program. It would be full of details on how many trucks (nicknamed the "great white fleet") were on the road traveling to how many streams carrying how many hundreds of thousands of trout, information eagerly awaited by many anglers. Several fishermen I know would cut out the story so they could track the fleets to make sure their favorite stream was getting its fair share.

If interest in the stocking schedule is keen in the pre-season, it can be nearly all-consuming for some fishermen once the season opens. "Truck followers"—individuals who shadow the stocking trucks so they can be the first ones on a freshly planted stretch of water and hopefully catch their limit before the trout realize they aren't in Kansas anymore—are well known to every trout angler. After decades of having the great white fleet shadowed and crowds turn wild at the sight of fresh trout, the commission in the 1980s decided to stop publicizing the dates and times of in-season stockings. The move angered some fishermen, but they adapted. The lack of specific information now cuts down on the craziness and gives the fish half a chance to acclimate themselves before they end up with freezer burn. Of course, the move did nothing to stop the really serious truck followers. I know guys who every season spend days riding up and down back roads, searching for the elusive stocking truck.

One stocking truck driver told me he once had a fisherman follow him a quarter of the way across Pennsylvania. The driver had just left the commission's hatchery in Pleasant Gap, Centre County, and was about to get on Interstate 80 when he noticed a car going the opposite way slam on its brakes, whip around, and start following him. Without even knowing if the truck even contained any fish or if it was just being driven to Pittsburgh or Erie for service, apparently, the fisherman trailed him west through most of Centre County and across Clearfield County to a stream in Jefferson County. When the truck reached its destination, the fisherman was clearly relieved, the driver said, because he was running out of gas.

Being mostly a solitary angler who long ago lost interest in limits, I still try to check the Sunday sports section of local newspapers for the stocking schedule. This is so I know which streams to avoid. Sometimes I forget, though, and then I pay for my lapse by being caught on a stream during stocking day.

At the parking lot at the end of the Game Lands' road, I find eleven more vehicles and six fishermen ringing the pool below the lot. A red pickup pulls up, followed by a couple on a motorcycle. The signs are clear, but the reality still tough to accept.

As the couple remove their helmets, I ask: "Did they stock today?"

"I don't know," the man answers. "We're not fishing. We just decided to take a ride up and see what was going on after we saw all the cars."

As the couple head up the road, I watch four fishermen pass

in muddy hip boots. I have to accept the fact, I've stumbled onto a stocking. For a moment, I consider leaving, but it is a beautiful day, sunny with temperatures in the low eighties, the best spring day so far, and it feels good to be outdoors. Then a breathless man carrying a bright blue rod appears and unlocks the rear of a blue truck parked nearby.

"Just startin'?" he asks.

"Yeah," I nod.

"You should have been here before," he says. "They was catchin' 'em like hell. It's slowed down now." I try to return his smile.

Aware that the season of the hatch has begun, I am anxious to get back on the water after being driven off Laurel Hill Creek by rain. Since the stream near the Irwin post office was dirty, I decide to try Dunbar Creek, in Fayette County, because its rocky bottom and forest surroundings often keep it clear when other streams are muddy. I'm right. The water is nearly perfect, just a little high and with the barest tint of green.

Once dressed, I head for the pool at the end of the road. Most people skip the pool because it's shallow and frequently disturbed by anglers crossing to the opposite bank, but it has treated me well over the years, and I hope its drawbacks will work in my favor—until it comes into view and I see five people circling it. I think then my best chance is the fast water across from the parking lot. Clogged with downed trees and overhanging branches, the stretch is even less fished than the crossing pool.

My guess is better this time. The stretch is empty. Hurriedly, I string up my rod, tie on an Elk Hair Caddis, and on my third cast hook a brookie, Dunbar's most abundant species. The fish makes me feel better about the day. Maybe things won't be so bad if I stick to out-of-the-way spots, I tell myself as the brookie swims away.

I look up to find a boy of about nineteen or twenty closing in. He comes straight at me, until he is no more than seven or eight feet away. Only then does he stop fishing, but just long enough to walk seven or eight feet around me, where he starts again as if I didn't exist. When the boy is gone, I turn back toward the pool to find that another fisherman, this one looks to be in his forties, has moved in. Then a second boy walks down to the stream, which puts three fishermen on about a ten-yard stretch of marginal water. I reel in line, hook my fly in the keeper ring, and climb up the bank.

Back on the road, I find the shallow water at the start of an upstream trail deserted. The stretch has a bare rock bottom, so it contains little food or cover to attract fish. With so many people ringing the pools, however, I decide it might have turned into a refuge.

Again my guess is good, and within a few minutes I hook and release two brookies. Then the punkies strike. The tiny, soft-bodied insects swarm like a cloud of soot around my head, up my nose, in my mouth and ears, down my shirt. I swat and wave at the mass, but this clears the air for only a few seconds. What I need is a cigar. Tobacco may be a killer, but cigar smoke is a sure cure for the biting, choking insects. Caught without a cigar, I rub insect repellant on my arms, face, neck, and ears. The chemical stops the punkies from landing, but it does nothing to halt their buzzing about my head.

Soon they are replaced by another nuisance. Two teenage boys who apparently saw me catch the fish have closed in on both sides of the stream. Like the boy in the fast water, they act as if I am invisible and drift their lines down in front of me to the spot where I took the brookies. Stunned by such bad manners, I can only watch openmouthed at first. Then I get angry and lay several casts close to their lines, once even briefly hooking the leader of the boy on the opposite bank, until I realize I am falling into their game.

Success being the best revenge, I notice the fish they want have dropped downstream and let out line so that my fly swings over the fish in their new holding spots. Within a minute, I take two more brookies, including one that is almost black. Then the kids' lines are back in front of me, swinging down toward the spot where I caught the fish. Only from where they are standing they cannot see they are fishing over bare rock. I back out of the stream, making sure I am not too careful about disturbing the water.

When I reach the deep pool with the undercut boulder a short distance upstream, I can't believe it's empty. It is one of the best pools on Dunbar Creek. The cave under the face of the rock always holds fish, and this time proves no exception. As soon as my fly lands on the surface a trout rises, but I move too fast and miss it, then miss it again. Four more fish rise to my flies in the pool, but none take. Then an old gentleman with white hair and an impeccably clean fishing vest appears at the upper end of the pool. I nod and continue to cast until he reaches me. Occasionally, an angler will appear on a stream who is more interested in talking than fishing. From the way the old fellow stands and watches, I suspect he might be one of these. Normally, I am more interested in fishing than talking, but since I've already done better than expected I don't mind a little small talk. I step up to the trail.

"You catch anything?" he asks.

"I got five and missed a few others," I tell him. I notice his rod is not strung.

"You fish this stream often?" he asks.

"Usually a couple times a year," I say. "How about you?"

"I used to fish it a lot years ago," he says, "but this is kind of a rough area back here. I don't want to get caught on the stream after dark. I just wanted to see the old place."

His voice carries a sense of longing that I understand. Once in a while, the urge to fish a stream I was very happy on but have not fished for years becomes overpowering. Every stream an angler fishes carries a part of his life. To return, even if it is just for a walk along the bank, is to possess what is gone again. For a morning or an afternoon a sixty-five-year-old or forty-year-old or a nineteen-year-old (real age makes no difference) can relive the past. They can recall the first trout they took on a fly, the best Green Drake hatch they ever knew, how spooky it felt to be on the water alone after dark, or even meet again with a friend or loved one who is gone.

"You see all of the fish in that hole down at the end of the road?" the old gentleman asks.

"No," I tell him. "There were too many guys down there. I didn't stop."

"There must be fifty fish in it," he says. We stand and stare at the water without saying anything until we both know it is time to move on.

From the pool with the boulder, I work my way upstream through the gaps in the crowd to a run above a small feeder stream where I miss another fish. Typically, the farther I get from the road the less people I see, but also the less fish. The fifty fish the old gentleman mentioned begin to prey on my mind. I look at my watch. It is almost seven-thirty. With any luck, most of the people at the pool will be gone, I think, and hurry back down the path.

When I reach the pool the situation is even better than I would have dreamed. It is empty. Quickly, I edge into the water alongside an overhanging branch, strip line off my reel, and start casting to what looks to be four or five fish holding near the center of the stream. None of the trout take my fly, but one after another they rise to consider it, until it is time to try something different. Over and over I cast to them, changing flies, and fish—sometimes bringing up one, sometimes another—until I am lost in the moment, a perfect part of my surroundings, the branch that hides me, the bird singing overhead, the rock on my left, the white moth fluttering away. I am a mink, an otter, a raccoon waiting my chance. So far gone in the moment am I that when an awkward splash breaks the spell I actually jump and turn to find two teenage boys.

When the smaller of the two boys spots me behind the branch, he startles, and then has the good manners to move off. The heavyset boy along the opposite bank, however, acts as if I am a tree. Without the slightest hesitation, he crawls up onto the rock directly above the fish I have been casting to and, after leaning out over the water to see if there is anything in the pool, starts to cast. His action is so blatant it annoys me. He has not stolen just a fishing spot from me, but a mood. I feel like grabbing the little bastard and throwing him into the pool. Although every season brings its share of encounters with rude fishermen, it has been years since I've run into anybody so aggressive and so blissfully unconcerned with the effects of his actions. Even embarrassed calls from his friend have no effect. Only after he stirs up every fish in the pool does he climb down from the rock and waddle off.

Freshly stocked trout are accustomed to people, and it takes only a few moments for the fish in the pool to settle down and begin feeding again. Before I can get off a cast, though, a man who looks to be in his late forties wades through the tail of the pool with two teenage boys in tow, climbs up on the same rock and leans out over the water. "Asshole," I say loud enough to be heard and then reel in my line and head for my car. For the first time since the start of my season I feel worse rather than better for having gone fishing.

Uncle Thad

He was known to his contemporaries as the "father of American angling" and today as the "American Walton." Angling historian John McDonald says he was the "great American fisher" of the nineteenth century, "learned in fishing literature and experienced in native practice. He knew about everything there was to know in his time, put it all down in 1864, and thereby equipped the school of early American fly-fishing with a rounded theory and practice." The founder of *Esquire* magazine, Arnold Gingrich calls him the "very prototype of the purely American breed of dry-fly men." Like McDonald, Gingrich sees him as one of the great American angling figures of the nineteenth century and believes a century from now he might stand alone. Even Theodore Gordon, who himself has been called the "American Cotton" and the "godfather of American fly fishing," acknowledged a debt, calling his book "my book of books for many years." Despite such acclaim, Thaddeus Norris's *The American Angler's Book: Embracing the Natural History of Sporting Fish, and the Art of Taking Them* is nearly impossible to find today outside of the special collections of libraries and rare book shops, and there is very little biographical information available on the author.

Among the very few writers who knew Norris is fish culture pioneer Fred Mather, who provides a glimpse of the man in his 1901 book, *My Angling Friends*. Mather says he became acquainted with Norris in 1868 when he bought a copy of Norris's lesser-known book *American Fish Culture*. "Just who he might be, or what he might know of the subject, I did not know, but it was the first publication of its kind that I had heard of." Mather met Norris for the first time in 1873 at a fisheries conference. Mather was then forty years old and Norris sixty-two, "a lovable old man whom many people called 'Uncle Thad,' and I soon dropped into the habit of addressing him so." After the meeting, Norris invited Mather to fish for perch with him at Betterton on Chesapeake Bay.

After a night spent at Norris's home in Philadelphia, during which time Uncle Thad "spread his heart wide open and captivated" Mather, the two men boarded a steamer for Delaware City. There they connected with the Chesapeake & Delaware Canal and continued on to Chesapeake City, and then down the Elk River into the bay. They reached Betterton at 4 A.M. "Neither of us grumbled—we made light of having to turn out at that time . . . as we walked up from the landing to the house where we were to stop, he said: 'The only thing I prefer to getting out of bed at 4 o'clock in the morning is sitting up all night.'"

After a four-hour nap while the tide turned, Mather and Norris left for the perch grounds, with the son of their host. They went armed with eight-foot bass rods, multiplier reels, shedder crabs, worms, and a dipsy of two ounces. "'Dipsy,' in the Philadelphia language, means a piece of wire to keep two hooks on short snells apart, and a sinker hangs at proper depth." They filled more than two bushels with perch that day. From conversations with the men in the roughly fifty other boats in the area, they "estimated the catch of the entire party that day at 6,000 white perch, besides a few other fishes . . . it was not a very good day for perch."

Out of this single trip grew a friendship that was to last until Norris's death. For a time Mather visited the older man every Tuesday evening at his home on Philadelphia's Logan Square. Norris's charm and humor are evident in many of the anecdotes Mather relates, among them is one about a pretentious fisherman from Pittsburgh who cornered Uncle Thad at the Philadelphia Centennial Exposition in 1876. Norris and Mather were observing a collection of fish in a tank "when a noisy sort of fellow introduced himself to Mr. Norris as 'a brother of the angle,' and after a long recital of his exploits, said: 'Yes, Mr. Norris, I'm the boss fisherman of western Pennsylvania, and I catch more fish than anyone else I ever met.'

"'I am always pleased to meet a thorough angler,' said Uncle Thad, very seriously. `I suppose you fish with a fly?'

"'Always, Mr. Norris; always.'

"'Always rig the rod properly with a float and sinker?'

"'Oh yes, always use the float and sinker.'

"'That's right; I see that you are really an expert angler, and I am glad to know you.'

"Mr. Norris never smiled, nor did his eye change when it met mine, and the man suspected nothing. After the man departed Uncle Thad said: 'I often meet such men, and I sized him up for a man who knew nothing of fly-fishing and would need a float and sinker if he tried to cast a fly.'"

Mather also mentioned that Norris was an accomplished banjo player who used an instrument without frets and had a vast repertoire of plantation songs from the antebellum South. What scant biographical information is available on Norris shows him to have been born in Culpeper, Virginia, on August 15, 1811. His family roots in America go back to 1630 when Thomas Norris emigrated from England to Maryland. According to Marjorie Butler Harrison, in *Pennsylvania Descendants of Thomas Norris of Maryland: 1630–1959*, he was one of six sons of Thaddeus Norris Senior and Ann Calvert, and he began his love affair with fishing as a child. "From boyhood on he had been an ardent lover of angling and in after years became an authority on the haunts, the habits and the instincts of fish."

Norris moved to Philadelphia in 1829, at the age of eighteen, and established himself as a successful merchant. Census records from 1860 describe him as a "clothier." Philadelphia city directories from his later years list him as a partner in a drug firm.

On January 17, 1837, Norris married Dorothea Abel. The couple lived in a house at 221 South Eighteen Street and had nine children, three of whom died in childhood and two others preceded their father in death. Dorothea Norris (sometimes also spelled Doratha) died at age thirty-eight of what the Philadelphia coroner describes as "cancer" on January 11, 1858. Norris remarried, possibly Dorothea's sister, Caroline Abel, but no date of marriage is available. The couple had no children and Norris died on April 11, 1877.

Those are the bare bones of the life of Thaddeus Norris. The obituary by his friend Joseph Townsend in the April 1877 issue of *Forest & Stream* captures something of his essence:

While in expertness, perseverance and keen relish for luring the wary trout to his fly he had few superiors, it was not by these that he made a trip in his company one long pleasure. The vista down the stream underneath o'erarching boughs; the sturdy or graceful forms of the various trees, according to their kind; the exquisite forms of vegetable life as shown in the mosses, ferns and lowly growths of the forest and along the margin of the stream; the aromatic balm of the air, laden with the resinous odors of spruce and hemlock; the habits of the birds and insects; the expressions and colors of the dawn and sunset; the changing face of a familiar landscape under varying skies, with alterations of lights and shadows—all these things fed his soul with joy. . . .

He was ever full of sympathy and encouragement for every novice in angling or tackle making who chose to appeal to his stores of useful knowledge for suggestions or aid. The boy who loved to go a-fishing always found the soft spot in his heart; and his love for children was as remarkable as his success in winning them to love him. He ever manifested the heartiest sympathy and respect for the worthy poor, and his sudden departure will be mourned in many a lowly home where the dwellers had their burdens lightened and their hearts cheered by a friend whose interest in their welfare they knew by an infallible instinct was genuine and sincere. . . .

His experience in angling was wide and varied. From the lordly salmon to the smallest member of the finny tribe, he had captured many varieties, and in many waters. But after all this experience was attained, he was ever ready to confess that his highest enjoyment from the sport was attained by an excursion with a congenial spirit to a mountain trout stream which he could wade, and along which he could wander at will, taking in due season his "nooning" and rest for the impromptu dinner, made up in good part from the morning catch, and where the pipe and sweet discourse which followed whiled away the time until the afternoon sun lowered to the proper point for beginning the evening fishing, which was protracted into the gloaming— this was, in his opinion, the crown of the angler's delight.

Although Mather's and Townsend's comments are evocative and interesting, neither illuminates the personality of Norris as well as his own writings, and none is more revealing than the introduction to *The American Angler's Book*, in which he lays out his thoughts on fishing and presents views that, as with all great literature, remain valid even today:

> But let me ask what is an angler, and who is a true angler? One who fishes with nets is not, neither is he who spears, snares, or dastardly uses the crazy bait to get fish, or who catches them on set lines; nor is he who boisterous, noisy, or quarrelsome; nor are those who profess to practice the higher branches of the art, and affect contempt for their more humble brethren, who have not attained their proficiency, imbued with the feeling that should possess the true angler.
>
> Nor is he who brings his ice-chest from town, and fishes all day with worm or fly, that he may return to the city and boastingly distribute his soaked and tasteless trout among his friends and brag of the numbers he has basketed, from fingerlings upwards.

Norris believed that anglers could be divided into almost as many categories as fish. His categories include the "Fussy Angler, a great bore"; the "Snob Angler," who knows it all; "The Greedy, Pushing Angler," who is always rushing ahead and crowding others; the "Spic-and-Span Angler," who is equipped with all the latest and most expensive tackle but does his best fishing indoors over a glass of whiskey; the "Rough-And-Ready Angler," who disdains all tomfoolery and carries his flies in a tangled mass; the "Literary Angler," who fishes mostly in books; the "Pretentious Angler," who despises anything about the sport that is not scientific.

The "True Angler," on the other hand, fishes for recreation, never quarrels with his luck, and can find amusement along a stream no matter what the fishing might be like. He is generally a modest man who does not force his thoughts upon others but is always ready to help. "He is moderately provided with all tackle and 'fixins' necessary to the fishing he is in pursuit of," quietly self-reliant, and ready for almost any emergency. He also enjoys the "accompaniment of the art":

> With happy memories of the past summer, he joins to-gether the three pieces of his fly-rod at home, when the scenes of last season's sport are wrapped in snow and ice, and renews the glad feelings of long summer days. With what interest he notes the swelling of the buds on the maples, or the advent of the blue-bird and robin, and looks forward to the day when he is to try another cast! and, when it comes at last, with what pleasing anticipations he packs up his "traps," and leaves his business cares and the noisy city behind, and after a few hours' or days' travel in the cars, and a few miles in a rough wagon, or a vigorous tramp over rugged hills or along the road that leads up the banks of the river, he arrives at his quarters! . . . How pleasingly rough everything looks after leaving the prim city! How pure and wholesome the air! How beautiful the clumps of sugar-maples and the veteran hemlocks jutting out over the stream; the laurel; the ivy; the moss-covered rocks; the lengthening shadows of evening! How musical the old familiar tinkling of the cow-bell and the cry of the whip-poor-will! How sweetly he is lulled to sleep as he hears "The waters leap and gush / O'er channelled rock, and broken bush!"
>
> Next morning, after a hearty breakfast of mashed potatoes, ham and eggs, and butter from the cream of the cow that browses in the woods, he is off, three miles up the creek, a cigar or his pipe in his mouth, his creel at his side, and his rod over his shoulder, chatting with his chum as he goes; free, joyous, happy; at peace with his Maker, with himself, and all mankind; he should be grateful for this much, even if he catches no fish. How exhilarating the music of the stream! how invigorating its waters, causing a consciousness of manly vigor, as he wades sturdily with the strong current and casts his flies before him! When his zeal abates, and a few of the *speckled* lie in the bottom of his

creel, he is not less interested in the wild flowers on the bank, or the scathed old hemlock on the cliff above, with its hawk's nest, the lady of the house likely inside, and the male proprietor perched high above on its dead top, and he breaks forth lustily—the scene suggesting the song—"The bee's on its wing, and the hawk on its nest, / And the river runs merrily by."

When noon comes on, and the trout rise lazily or merely nip, he halts "sub tegmine fagi," or under the shadow of the dark sugar-maple to build a fire and roast trout for his dinner, and wiles away three hours or so. He dines sumptuously, straightens and dries his leader and the gut of his dropper, and repairs all breakage. He smokes leisurely, or even takes a nap on the green sward or velvety moss, and resumes his sport when the sun has declined enough to shade at least one side of the stream, and pleas- antly anticipates the late evening cast on the still waters far down the creek. God be with you, gentle angler, if actuated with the feeling of our old master! whether you are a top fisher or a bottom fisher; whether your bait be gentles, brandling, grub, or red worm; crab shrimp, or minnows; caddis, grasshopper, or the feathery counterfeit of the ephemera, may your thoughts always be peaceful, and your heart filled with gratitude to Him who made the country and the rivers; and "may the east wind never blow when you go fishing!"

No Life So Happy

Spurred by memories awakened by the old gentleman on Dunbar Creek and a nagging need to restore my faith in fishing, two days after getting caught in the stocking frenzy I decide to give in to an urge that has been simmering in me for a couple of seasons— to return to Clear Shade Creek. For three seasons in my mid-twenties, on a regular basis, I made the seventy-five-mile trip from my home to that northern Somerset County water. Friends who aren't fishermen thought I was crazy to travel so far for only an afternoon or a morning of fishing. Their remarks just made me smile. They had no idea what I had found, and I wasn't quick to share it.

The small tourist publication that alerted me to Clear Shade called it one of the finest trout streams in the region and, typical for such publications, pointed as proof to the number of fish stocked in it. What really caught my attention was the stream's isolation. Its Fly-Fishing-Only Project was about two miles from the nearest paved road. It seemed impossible that such a place could exist in western Pennsylvania. I imagined Hemingway's Nick Adams on the Big Two-Hearted River.

My first trip to Clear Shade was far less exciting than my imagination had painted. It was on a Sunday afternoon drive with a girlfriend, and we didn't fish, we just looked. A week later we were back, weaving and stumbling our way upstream over rocks, eroded banks, and assorted deadfalls to catch a couple of small brookies. We did it without seeing another soul.

When I reach the mouth of Clear Shade Creek, I am surprised to find the gate leading to the Windber Water Authority Dam open. The cinder road guarded by the gate is the easiest way to reach Clear Shade's Fly Fishing Only water. But as many times as I've been to the stream, I've never seen the gate open. I don't know what to do. The idea of driving back to the project is tempting, but I don't want to return and find the gate locked. I guess a work crew is at the dam and decide to drive back and ask permission to park. About a mile up the road a knot of men and equipment blocks the way. They are working on a water tank. When I ask to park, the foreman shrugs and simply tells me to pull off the road and be out by four o'clock. Thrilled with my luck, I glance at my watch; it's not quite one o'clock. Three hours is enough fishing time, especially when measured against a two-mile walk both in and out.

The blazes I cut on trees along the road my last season on the stream are long gone, so I have no idea where I might strike water as I start into the woods. When it turns out to be the pool where my friend Art once caught eight trout without moving a step, I almost shout for joy. But this time the pool is not nearly so cooperative. Not a fish moves in it or in the next one or in the one above it, where I once caught five beautiful brown trout. Then, at the last pool below the dam, my line hangs up on a piece of brush and I finally spot a fish. He is holding in an opening protected by a latticework of roots. Untangling the line, I step back and try to dab my fly into the opening. Brush grabs my leader every time the fly nears the water, until I hook a root and the fish dashes for cover, leaving me feeling clumsy and regretful.

Pennsylvania's mountainous topography makes reclusive lakes a rarity in most locations, so the Windber Water Authority Dam has always fascinated me. Being a municipal water supply, it is closed to fishing. As I pass, all I can do is dream about the giant trout I imagine living in it and continue on to the wire marking the downstream end of the Fly-Fishing-Only water, where I crawl up onto the boulder above the first pool.

I know that looking for trout from atop a boulder is stupid, but sometimes it is just as important to see fish as to catch them. Besides, the rock is where I want to be. It is the same spot where one October I teased trout after trout up from the bottom of the stream. They chased everything that day, including an ungodly pink Girdle Bug that a magazine story told me worked in the fall.

Now, however, several minutes of watching reveals nothing. Disappointed, I am ready to move on, when twin flashes of gold at the tail of the pool catch my eye. I jump down off the boulder (noticing that the landing has become harder over the past decade), then circle downstream of the flashes and into a casting spot where I find not two, but a half dozen trout.

My first casts send the fish wildly darting back and forth across the stream. They turn to look, rise, and place their noses on my fly, follow, and then decide better. I become so used to refusals and lethargic in my actions, that when one finally goes for my fly I react by yanking it away. "Son of a bitch!" I shout, but the curse is more of a call to action than anger. I expect another chance, and it comes a few seconds later when a fish explodes out of the current along the opposite bank. I turn him before he can reach the safety of the boulder and then, after a short downstream run, bring him in, an average brookie.

Although there is nothing extraordinary about the fish, catching it relieves something that has been pressing on me since Dunbar Creek. After releasing it, I try a few more casts. Then I give up and stretch out on the bank to watch the sky, and Edwin Peterson slips into my mind.

Peterson was an English professor at the University of Pittsburgh who died in 1972. He is best known for his book *Penn's Wood West*, a prose and photographic journey through 1950s western Pennsylvania. Relatively few people are aware that Peterson also wrote another book with western Pennsylvania as the setting. He published the novel *No Life So Happy* in 1940. It tells the story of a mysterious fishing trip taken by a nameless narrator and his friend to the Shade watershed during the Great Depression. My friend Jan Caveney, a waterways conservation officer with the Fish and Boat Commission, told me about the book. Jan has the best collection of angling books of anybody I know, well over fifteen hundred volumes, and calls *No Life So Happy* one of the best he has ever read.

Such a powerful recommendation caused me to dig out a copy of the novel from the Carnegie Library. It is an unusual mix of love, philosophy, friendship, fishing, mysticism, and possible murder. It may be the strangest angling book I've ever read, a rare work of outdoor literature from an abused land and full of wonderful writing:

> Those first few minutes on the stream are important. We pretend, of course, that we are looking for signs—what kind of hatches, if any, are on the water; what kind of rises. . . . But actually, the signs are incidental. We are alone on the edge of running water, singing water. It seems to move gently through our whole body. Muscles relax, the mind clears. Overhead a few wisps of gray cloud dissolve and the blue comes through. Sunlight brightens the top of a scraggly pine and the grass at our feet is gray with dew. There is the smell of fresh earth and of winter-green that the snow has not killed. Across the stream a chickadee does acrobatics on the end of a budding twig. The air is clean and good. Day broadens, and with it things within ourselves.

Closing my eyes, I feel the breeze across my face and listen to the rustle of the leaves, and then the call of a bird. I wish I could identify more birds by their calls—or more birds, period. Like wild flowers, they are becoming more interesting to me every season.

A Matter of Philosophy

⁓

In the Native American's view of the universe, animals were brothers, fellow travelers on the river of life. *Wild* was an unknown word. There was only the Earth and the creatures who lived upon it. Deer, bear, elk, bass, salmon, and trout gave their lives when hunted or caught so their Indian brothers might live. The Native American in turn thanked them and honored their spirits through various rituals and celebrations. The Seneca Billy Shongo explains the Native American's point of view in Henry Shoemaker's *Black Forest Souvenirs*, a collection of stories from northern Pennsylvania:

> One of our wise men, in advising us to keep out of farming put it this way, "You ask me to plow the ground! Shall I take a knife and tear my mother's bosom? Then when I die she will not take me to her bosom to rest. You ask me to grub out stones! Shall I dig under her skin for bones? Then when I die I cannot enter her body to be born again. You ask me to cut grass and make hay and sell it, and be rich like white men! But how dare I cut off my mother's hair?"

By contrast, European settlers saw wildlife and the Earth as objects, mainly as ways to accumulate wealth. In their eyes, the new continent was a horn of plenty to be exploited in whatever fashion they saw fit. They lived in a world that believed almost without challenge that the Earth had been created in six twenty-four-hour days and that humans were God's highest achievement, created in His image and given the Earth to use as they saw fit. As one nineteenth-century pioneer put it: "The good Lord put us here and the Good Book says, 'man shall have dominion over all creatures.' They're ourn to use."

In *Triumphant Democracy,* Andrew Carnegie reduced the whole of nature to mere facts and figures. Eastern Pennsylvania was anthracite coal waiting to be dug and sold: "Near Pottsville there is a thickness of 3,300 feet of coal measures. The cubic contents of the anthracite coal field, allowing fifty per cent for loss working, is estimated at 13,180,535,000 tons of merchantable coal." Western Pennsylvania's rivers in Carnegie's mind were cheap transportation: "Take the Ohio . . . a competent authority has stated that the total of its trade from its head at Pittsburg to its mouth at New Cairo . . . exceeded in 1874 $800,000,000. . . . Coal, coke, and other bulky articles are transported at the rate of one-twentieth of a cent., one fortieth of a penny per ton of mile." Conquering nature was viewed as a religion by Carnegie:

Auguste Comte has gravely propounded a religion of humanity which he says is worshipful because of its victories over nature. There have been religions founded on less worthy grounds than these. Man has indeed played a wonderful part in the world; and nothing can be more marvelous than the way in which he has subjugated the forces of nature, and yoked them to his chariot and his boat.

At the same time Carnegie was preaching the conquest of nature, however, he also must have felt a hint of what his times would look like to future generations. He notes: "'As one man's meat is another man's poison,' so one age's civilization is the next age's barbarism. We shall all be barbarians to our great, great, grandchildren."

Following their beliefs and because of their low numbers, Native Americans were able to live in relative harmony with Pennsylvania's water, fish, and wildlife for about sixteen thousand years—or until Europeans arrived and lured them away from their successful lifestyle with a collection of second-rate pots, blankets, beads, knives, whiskey, and promises of a better life. Driven by greed and claiming justification in the Bible, it took European settlers only about two hundred years after William Penn's arrival to decimate Pennsylvania's waters—to such an extent that many species became extinct and thousands of miles of rivers and streams flowed discolored, stinking, and barren. Records of the Howell family of Woodbury, New Jersey, tell the tale of shad in the Delaware River: "Prior to 1825, the average annual returns were about 130,000; from 1845 to 1849, the average fell to 66,890; from 1866 to 1869, the average catches were 60,739; from 1870 to 1873 the yearly average was less than 25,000."

The situation was just as gloomy on the Susquehanna and Juniata Rivers. In May 1829 shad appeared in the Juniata River in numbers greater "than has ever been known at any previous time," according to the *Mifflin Eagle*. This abundance ended the following year when the Tide Water Canal Company built a dam on the Susquehanna River at Columbia and cut off the shad runs. The dam convinced people living below it that the shad were doomed and they had better get their share. "They threw all discretion to the winds, and adopted all kinds of outrageous methods of taking fishing," Fish Commission reports of the time note. Between every rock in the Susquehanna they anchored fish baskets until the river was essentially fenced. Even in remote regions, market fishing quickly took hold. Philip Tome in his book *Pioneer Life* (1854) mentions the scarcity of fish and game around the Jersey Shore at the confluence of Pine Creek and the West Branch Susquehanna River as early as the 1790s: "Fish and venison being so abundant in the vicinity where we lived [Slate Run], and very scarce at the mouth of Pine Creek . . . we used them as articles of traffic . . . by exchanging them with the inhabitants there."

It was not only settlers with nets, weirs, and baskets who were wreaking havoc on fish populations, however. Long rods and flies were routinely used to supply fish for market. Genio Scott in his 1869 work, *Fishing in American Waters*, notes: "On Pine Creek, in Pennsylvania, anglers who fish for a livelihood use such a rod [twelve feet long], and fish with only one clumsily-tied fly. They wade the stream . . . and to a string tied over the left shoulder and under the left arm they attach their fish, and tow them along as they angle down the stream. On some days they take from thirty to fifty pounds of trout."

In his 1819 book, *Letters from the British Settlement in Pennsylvania*, C. B. Johnson provides another example of abundance and greed in northeastern Pennsylvania: "Trout abound in them [the region's rivers], as may be best seen by the result of a day's fishing with rod and line, in the outlet of Silver lake, by two gentlemen, at three different times. The first time, they caught twenty-seven dozen; the second time, twenty dozen; and the third time, thirty-five dozen and a half."

The damage unregulated fishing inflicted upon Pennsylvania's fisheries was more or less temporary and correctable, as long as clean water remained available, through laws and restocking efforts. The problems early settlers caused were relatively small compared to the destruction brought by the sacrifice of the state to the Industrial Revolution.

King Coal, the fossil remains of the tropical forests that once covered Pennsylvania, is the foundation upon which much of the state's history rests. About one-third of Pennsylvania is underlain by coal. The Pittsburgh seam of bituminous coal has been called the single most important mineral deposit in the world. At one time a full quarter of the total coal output of North America came from the anthracite region of eastern Pennsylvania. The earliest suggestion that coal might be found in Pennsylvania was made in 1698, when the Quaker Gabriel Thomas noted of the country between Philadelphia and the Susquehanna River: "And I have reason to believe there are good Coals also, for I observ'd, the Runs of Water have the same Colour as that which proceeds from the Coal-Mines in Wales." The first record of coal in the state appears on a map made by trader John Pattin in 1752. It shows the Freeport Seam along the Kiskiminetas River in western Pennsylvania.

Well supplied with coal from Great Britain, the early Quakers never bothered searching for the mineral. The first record of anthracite coal in Pennsylvania does not appear until 1762, when John Jenkins, a surveyor for the Susquehanna Company, noted two outcroppings of "stone coal" near Wilkes-Barre. During the eighteenth century, coal was little used except by blacksmiths and as fuel by people who lived in areas where it was easily obtainable. The Gore brothers, Wilkes-Barre blacksmiths, are credited with being the first to use the difficult-to-burn anthracite for fuel in 1769. By 1820 anthracite was a staple on the domestic scene and was being regularly shipped down the Delaware River.

A similar situation developed in the bituminous fields of western Pennsylvania. The Reverend Charles Beatty provides an account of the way the environment was disregarded for coal on Mount Washington above downtown Pittsburgh, in 1766:

> A fire being made by the workmen not far from the place where they dug coal, and left burning when they went away, by the small dust communicated itself to the body of the coals and set it on fire, and has now been burning almost a twelve months entirely under ground. . . . The fire has already undermined some part of the mountain so that great fragments of it, and trees with their roots are fallen down its face.

Pittsburgh also is the source of an early complaint about air pollution. It appeared in the June 10, 1814, issue of the *Pittsburgh Gazette* in the form of a letter by "One of the people." The author writes:

> Although much of the prosperity is owing to its "Fires," it is not to be concealed, that the effects of those immense fires, have become subjects of complaint. That the evil (if it be an evil to be enveloped in smoke) is daily increasing, and that relief is now universally called for. To such in our day and generation, as appear to have been raised in the nurture and admonition, of the Prince of the power of the Air, there may be consolation, from the hope, that initiated here in infernal habits, and familiarized to blazes, heat, smoke, soot and the blackness of darkness in this life, the transition to that which is to come, will be easy, and Hell thus stripped of its terrors.

King Coal's devouring of Pennsylvania can be seen in production records. In 1800, about 87,000 tons of bituminous coal and 250 tons of anthracite were mined in the state. By 1850, those figures had been pushed to 2.1 million tons bituminous and 4.3

million tons anthracite. Twenty-five years later, the figures had climbed to 23 million tons anthracite and 12.5 million tons bituminous, and by 1900 to more than 57 million tons anthracite and 77 million ton bituminous. Anthracite output peaked during World War I at 99.6 million tons and bituminous in 1925 at 178 million tons.

From coal grew the iron, steel, and lumber industries, the canals, and the railroads. Thomas Rutter, a blacksmith and Quaker minister, constructed the state's first ironworks on Manatawny Creek, Montgomery County, in 1718. By the start of the American Revolution, North America was producing more iron than England, and most of it was coming from eastern Pennsylvania. More than eighty furnaces and other iron-making facilities were built in the state between 1716 and 1776. By 1810, there were 44 blast furnaces, 78 forges, 50 plating mills, 18 slitting mills, 175 naileries, and an undetermined number of bloomeries and air furnaces.

At first, the role of rivers and streams in the manufacture of iron was limited to supplying power to operate the bellows and for cooling purposes. The effects of the early furnaces on the environment was detrimental, but the country was so immense and empty that the land easily absorbed the punishment. As the industry grew and the forests surrounding the furnaces were cut for fuel, though, the need for coal increased. To meet demands, more mines appeared, and more canals to carry the coal to market. The Schuylkill Canal, opened in 1825, was the first of a series of canals built across the state between the 1820s and the 1840s, in a system that altered stream flows and destroyed hundreds of miles of fish habitat.

Following the iron furnaces and canals came the railroads, steel mills, the lumber and oil industries. The *Stourbridge Lion,* the first locomotive to operate in the Western Hemisphere, made its first run at Honesdale, Wayne County, on August 8, 1829. By the opening salvos of the Civil War, there were twenty railroads in Pennsylvania. Eventually, some sixty railroads would operate in the state on some eleven thousand miles of track.

Floodplains being the only level land in most of Pennsylvania, railroads routinely followed the course of rivers and streams and encouraged ridership by promoting fishing in waters along their tracks. An 1883 brochure by the Pennsylvania Railroad

Company announces "A Paradise for Gunners and Anglers." Some railroads even offered prizes for the largest fish caught along its route. Combined with an absence of regulations, the pressure exerted by thousands of anglers proved to be more than many waterways could bear, and fish numbers rapidly declined.

Even more destructive to Pennsylvania's fisheries than the access provided by the railroads was their opening up of more of the state to mining, timber, and other industries. By the start of the Civil War, the mills were turning out more than half the five hundred thousand tons of rolled iron being produced annually in the United States. Samuel Nutt built the first steel mill in Pennsylvania in Chester County in 1732, but like early ironworks, it was a small affair. During the 1850s, large rolling mills for iron rails began operating at Danville on the Susquehanna River, Phoenixville on the Schuylkill River, and Brady's Bend on the Allegheny River. Steel began to affect the state's environment in the 1860s and 1870s, when the Pennsylvania Steel Company at Steelton on the Susquehanna River, Freedom Iron & Steel Works at Lewistown on the Juniata River, and the Cambria Iron Company at Johnstown on the Conemaugh River all appeared. These first large mills were quickly joined by the gigantic Edgar Thomson Works in Homestead and Duquesne Works in Duquesne, both on the Monongahela River, and others on the Ohio, Allegheny, and Lehigh Rivers, all of which would on a daily basis indiscriminately dump millions of gallons of toxic waste into the state's rivers.

The steel industry's effect went far beyond the immediate site of the mills. Coke required so much water to produce that coal operators established their own water companies. In 1889, according to *The Inside History of the Carnegie Steel Company* by James Bridge, the H. C. Frick Coal & Coke Company alone had "three water plants with a pumping capacity of 5,000,000 gallons daily." Again, wastewater was simply allowed to run off into the nearest stream or river.

The same was true with the oil industry in northwestern Pennsylvania. For roughly half a century after Edwin Drake sank the world's first well drilled specifically for oil along Oil Creek at Titusville in 1859, thick crude was spilled and refinery waste released into the Allegheny River watershed. The region's waters were so thickly covered with petroleum and petroleum wastes that they actually caught fire on occasion. One blaze along Pithole Creek on June 19, 1865, required more than two hundred men to extinguish it. Thomas Roberts, an engineer with the U.S. Army Corps of Engineers, noted of the Allegheny in the 1870s:

> The horses employed by guiper [barrage] men in seasons of low water in towing boats . . . become smeared with tar refuse from oil refineries and acid works, while in other places the unfortunate animals have their legs cut with acid. This acid, refuse of vitriol, diluted as it is in the river, still accumulates in places sufficiently concentrated to disintegrate the fibers of cable, which frequently break as though cut through with a knife.

Supporting the mines, iron furnaces, steel mills, railroads, canals, and all the rest of it was the lumber industry. Pennsylvania's original forests practically covered the entire state. Although the Indians and early settlers cleared land to build their homes, fuel their fires, and plant their crops, and industry later used large quantities of trees to heat their furnaces and support their infrastructure, transportation difficulties restricted lumbering to areas near the streams and rivers on which logs could be floated to market. The forests of the interior were generally safe until the 1880s, when powerful locomotives and cranes were developed that were capable of climbing the state's mountains and hauling timber out of even the most remote valleys. The result was that between about 1880 and 1920, nearly all of Pennsylvania was clear-cut. Williamsport alone would see almost 225 million board feet of pine and hemlock pass through its boom on the West Branch Susquehanna annually. Photographs from the period show entire mountains denuded of trees. Logs were often left to rot when prices dropped or there was too much snow or not enough rain to transport them to market. At the mills, trimmings were disposed of by burning and the ash and sawdust dumped into the rivers and streams. Theodore Gordon wrote in a 1907 article in *Forest & Stream*:

> How we detest a sawmill on one of our favorite streams! The sappy, heavy sawdust not only floats on the surface, but sinks to the bottom and permeates the entire river. The

trout will not rise, in fact, I do not believe that natural flies would be noticed, even if they would come up through the trash, and hatch out on the surface. Those sawmills are responsible for many muttered bad words, and for several melancholy days.

The effects of industrial development on Pennsylvania's waterways and fish are vividly depicted in Charles Lose's 1928 work, *The Vanishing Trout*. Lose lived in Montoursville, Lycoming County. He focuses on the waters around his home, but what he describes could apply to every other watershed in the state by the end of World War I:

> From the mouth of the Sinnemahoning eastward to Williamsport, river fishing is a thing of the past. Stream abuse has killed the fish and destroyed the fishing. Even the eels have found their passage through this water attended with such danger that they have, for the most part, abandoned it for cleaner and purer waterways; and the lampreys imbedded in the mud at the bottom have all succumbed to the deadly poison.

In the West Branch, Lose watched fish being pushed farther and farther downstream by acid mine drainage and tannery effluvium until they were confined to a few miles of river below Williamsport where the pollution was diluted enough to allow them to breathe. Not even there were they safe, however. During high-water periods that increased acid drainage or when tanneries discharged their vats into the river, he often found fish crowding into small tributary streams in search of clean water.

What makes the destruction of Pennsylvania's land, water, and forests even worse than the record shows is that things could have been different. Lose tells of a Sullivan County tannery that operated for forty years without adverse effects on a nearby stream:

> A deep pool of the Loyalsock has always been the receptacle of the liquid coming from the tannery; yet this pool has never been shunned by either the trout or the bass. The precautions taken to prevent the destruction of fish was simple and inexpensive. Several beds containing ashes

received, one after the other, the sewage as it came from the tannery and cleansed it so that it could be safely run into the stream. . . . Such steps cost them little and interfered with the work of the tannery not at all. Fair profits from industrial plants and full fish baskets are not incompatible.

Other tanneries, mines, and mills could have treated their wastewater using such simple methods and the forests could have been cut in a sustainable and less wasteful manner that didn't leave valuable trees to rot on the ground. Even the smoke that earned Pittsburgh the name Smoky City could have been controlled at minimal cost. In the same 1814 letter in which he complained about the city's atmosphere, "One of the people" noted that a method had been developed by the English firm of Bolton & Watt for "consuming the smoke of furnaces, etc. adapted to any boiler or copper already set up, at a very small expense, without requiring more coal than usual."

In the Land of Heart-Shaped Bathtubs

The climax of the season of the hatch in Pennsylvania, the pinnacle of the fishing year for many anglers, comes in May and early June when they migrate from Pittsburgh and Philadelphia to the fertile waters of the northern mountains, their heads crammed full of visions of mayflies and rising trout. They make the trip for single days, starting out well before dawn and returning pleasantly exhausted well after dark, and for weekends, lengthened by nonexistent illnesses. A few lucky ones with enough foresight and seniority to arrange vacations even manage to make it to the mountains for an entire week.

My first trip of the season was set when Tom Prusak, a friend from the Pittsburgh Fly Fishers Club, invited me to the Pocono Mountains with him and Jack Hess, another friend from the club. Employment had forced Tom's son, Young Tom, to leave Pittsburgh for Philadelphia several years previously, and ever since then he had been trying to lure his dad east with tales of abundant hatches and willing trout. The offer finally became too sweet to resist when Young Tom's neighbor offered them the use of their family cottage near Hickory Run State Park.

Technically, the term *mountains* is a misnomer when applied to the Poconos. *Plateau* would be the proper term for the high country centered around northwestern Monroe County, but the term *mountains* has been used for so long, anything else sounds wrong. It would be like calling a brookie a trout, even though it's really a char. Geology aside, one fact about which there is no confusion is that the Poconos possess one of the most colorful sport-fishing traditions of any place in the United States. Angling writer and historian Ernest Schwiebert says the Poconos are "probably the true wellspring of American trout-fishing tradition."

The genesis of the Poconos as a holiday destination—the honeymoon land of heart-shaped bathtubs—goes back to about 1820 when residents of Philadelphia and New York began visiting the Delaware Water Gap near Stroudsburg. Sensing a profit in the numbers of visitors, Antoine Dutot, a French refugee from Santo Domingo, in 1829 started taking in travelers. Three years later, Samuel Snyder purchased property above the Delaware River and the following year opened the Kittatinny House, the region's first summer hotel.

Some guests of the Kittatinny undoubtedly spent their holiday fishing. But the Pocono angling tradition really took root at the inn built by Arthur Henry in 1836, halfway between Easton and Scranton on the Paradise Branch of Brodheads Creek. The log inn started out with a clientele of drovers, lumbermen, ice workers, hunters, and fishermen but gradually attracted more and more anglers, until Henry expanded the building in 1848, named it Henryville House, and began catering specifically to anglers.

The Poconos became a popular sport fishing center largely because of their location about one hundred miles between Philadelphia and New York. Their proximity to the New York publishing houses brought a great deal of publicity. Then, too, their streams contained good hatches of aquatic insects and large numbers of native brook trout, to which were added several stockings of brown trout in 1889. The combination, later aided by railroads offering cheap excursion fares, had anglers flocking to the Poconos by the late 1840s.

Joseph Jefferson, an avid angler, author of the play *Rip Van Winkle,* and the most famous actor of the early nineteenth century, summed up the attraction of Paradise Valley when he wrote: "A ridge of hills covered with tall hemlocks surrounds the vale, and numerous trout-streams wind through the meadows and tumble over the rocks. . . . The valley harmonized with me and our resources. The scene was wild, the air was fresh, and the board was cheap."

Jefferson was among the earliest of dozens of prominent artists, writers, politicians, military leaders, businessmen, industrialists, and religious leaders who made regular pilgrimages to the Poconos during the nineteenth century. Others included heavyweight boxing legend John L. Sullivan, Civil War hero General Phillip Sheridan, and Buffalo Bill and Annie Oakley. Gifford Pinchot—former governor of Pennsylvania, first head of the U.S. Forest Service, and author of *Let's Go Fishing* and *Just Fishing Talk*—made his home in Milford, Pike County, and frequently fished in the region. Among his angling companions was Teddy Roosevelt. Calvin Coolidge fished the Poconos, as did Grover Cleveland and Benjamin Harrison, who, incredibly, were both registered at Henryville House for a week before they were pitted against each other in the 1880 election.

The Poconos have been a magnet for fishing innovators, even more than for politicians and celebrities. Few regions have drawn so many well-known, important angling authors. Practically every writer of note has fished the region. The list of names runs like a who's who of angling literature, beginning with the Reverend George Washington Bethune, editor of the first American edition of *The Compleat Angler* (published in 1847), and Henry William Herbert, who under the pen name Frank Forester became the most popular sporting writer of pre–Civil War America.

Following Bethune and Forester came Teddy Roosevelt's uncle Robert Barnwell Roosevelt, author of *Game Fish of the Northern States of America and British Provinces,* and Thaddeus Norris, who frequently traveled to the Brodheads with Easton native Samuel Phillippe, developer of the six-strip bamboo rod. Other anglers of note who have fished the Poconos include George La Branche, Edward Ringwood Hewitt, the Reverend Henry Van Dyke, Sparse Grey Hackle, John Taintor Foote, Eugene Connett, Charles Wetzel, Dana Lamb, James Leisenring, Preston Jennings, Ed Zern, Charles Ritz, Arnold Gingrich, and Charlie Fox.

The Civil War brought a decline in fishermen to the Poconos followed by a near explosion of anglers, spurred both by joy at the end of the war and by cholera outbreaks in Philadelphia and New York. Tavern licenses were granted to forty-eight establishments in Monroe County in 1866. Then, in the mid-1870s, the railroads began promoting express service to the Poconos and the area was on its way to becoming one of the best-known vacation spots in the Northeast.

Hickory Run State Park grew out of a donation of twelve thousand acres to the National Park Service by Allentown businessman Harry Trexler in the 1930s. Like the Poconos as a whole, it had been part of the Walking Purchase of 1737, one of the first great swindles of Indian lands in American history. The purchase was supposedly based on a 1683 treaty, in which the Delawares agreed to sell the Penn Family all land within a boundary running from Wrightstown, Bucks County, parallel to the Delaware River as far as a man could walk in a day and a half.

Accustomed to hunting and resting on their travels, the Delawares expected the Europeans to walk only twenty-five or thirty miles through the rugged and unfamiliar country. Settlers, however, sent out survey crews to notch a trail, and then recruited the three fastest walkers available. In the end, the walk covered over sixty miles. To encompass even more land, the line that was to be drawn from the point where the farthest walker stopped east to the Delaware River was set at an angle that carried it north to about Lackawaxen, Pike County.

Early travelers gave the land on which the Hickory Run State Park stands the name Shades of Death, because of the virgin growths of hemlock and white pine dense enough to block out the sun. Clear-cut lumbering had made the title irrelevant already by the mid-1870s—which does not seem so bad an effect to me when a branch swings back, knocks off my hat, and smothers my face in leaves and spider webs. "Tom's really going to pay for this one!" I shout.

The plan, hatched by Young Tom the previous evening, called for Barry Fichtner and Todd Kern (two of his friends from the Philadelphia area) and I to fish Hayes Run, while Old Tom, Jack, and he headed for Hickory Run. "The path runs straight down to the stream," Young Tom had said, leaving us totally unprepared for "Times Square in the Woods," a clearing a hundred yards from the car, with trails running in practically every imaginable direction.

Thinking any turn might leave us hopelessly lost, we agree to continue straight ahead. When we reach a small pond (something Young Tom never mentioned), we decide to strike off through the woods, down a trickle of water we hope will lead to the stream. Ducking, bending, weaving, and twisting our way through blueberry, alder, birch, laurel, and greenbriers, we follow the ditch until it disappears into a bog of mud and moss, leaving us little choice but to plow ahead. When we finally hear water, it is at the bottom of a ledge so thick with rhododendron we can't even glimpse it. Driven by the longing to fish, and the stream sounds closer and closer the longer we stare at the rhododendron, but nowhere can we find an opening that looks large enough even for a rabbit. Reluctantly, we turn back into the woods and fight our way through the undergrowth until we stumble out into a floodplain next to a flat, clear pool.

Medium-size streams of about thirty feet in width have always been my favorite waters. I generally shy away from small streams because I find them too confining. So, when I look at Hayes Run my heart sinks; it's not exactly tiny, maybe ten or twelve feet wide, but it is heavy with brush. It will require a lot of sneaking and back-aching bending to catch the wild browns we were told fill it, maneuvers I'm not mentally prepared for after a season that so far has centered on larger water and newly planted hatchery trout.

State of mind generally being a sure way to success or failure, my third cast catches an alder and causes two dark shadows to dart out from under the bank. A second later, my back cast hooks another branch and drives away a third shadow. Four more times I tangle with the brush, knocking debris into the water and scattering shadows, until I stumble over a submerged rock and end all chances in that pool.

Downstream, Hayes Run eventually becomes a scenic stream of flat pools, rocky runs, and waterfalls framed by lush growths of grass, shrubs, rhododendron, pine, and hardwoods, but I am caught in a mind-set that wants it to be larger. I continue to spook the fish and my confidence fades. A single yellow stonefly flutters past and a trout rises against the far bank. I tie on a Yellow Sally and lay cast after cast over the spot even though I know my actions are probably scaring the wits out of every trout in the pool. I switch to a grasshopper, a trick a friend who loves tiny streams has used with great success—a big hunk of food for small water. Not this time, though.

Unfettered by expectations, Barry and Todd have done well, I learn when I reach them a half hour later. One took seven, the other five. Their success becomes embarrassing when I mention the size of the stream and they both say it's a treat compared to what they usually fish. This remark kills what is left of my desire, and I settle for watching Barry and Todd take several more colorful little brookies. Then someone mentions lunch. Not about to retrace our path to the stream, we decide to simply try heading uphill, and we find a trail only twenty-five yards from the water. Within minutes we are standing in Times Square.

"Yeah, but Tom's still going to hear about it," Barry says.

Although I dislike competition when it comes to angling, before my line tightens a few times I can be as aggressive as any guy trying to make a payment on a $25,000 bass boat by winning a tournament. It is always easier to be generous and noncompetitive when you are successful. As we eat lunch above Hickory Run, I can feel the pressure. Everybody has caught fish except me. When Young Tom attempts to soothe me by pointing out that "Hayes is tough," it only makes things worse. It is all I can do to manage a few weak jabs when Barry and Todd bring up Times Square. I finish my sandwich, grab my rod, and head for the water.

Crowded with brush, overhung with branches, and jammed with logs and rocks, Hickory Run is much the same as Hayes Run, but now I am ready. Up and down the bank my eyes search for open areas through which to lay a cast. Then I glance down to find a fish rising in the fast water almost at my feet.

Backing away from the bank, I move down the trail, across the stream, and up a gravel bar to a casting spot. As I work out line, the fish rises a second and a third time. It seems too good to be true, at least until my first cast drops a foot short, as does my second, and my third. My timing is horrible. Trying to adjust, I make a cast that appears too far, but it is taken instantly. I can't believe the fish was lying so far ahead of its rise. I am still puzzled when another splash comes from the original spot and I realize I've hooked a different fish, one that is all of four inches. But the bad spell is broken.

Minutes later I take the original fish, and then another, a gorgeous ten-inch brookie with a bright orange belly and razor sharp white-lined fins. I follow it up with two more from a long pool upstream. When Young Tom appears, I call to him with a friendliness I lacked at lunch and we fill each other in on our catches. Then he mentions Hayes Run.

"I can't believe you guys couldn't find it," he says.

"Well, if we had a guide who knew what he was talking about," I tease. "We just think it's awful suspicious you didn't want your dad or Jack going up there."

"Aw, come on. You guys don't really think I'd set you up?"

"All I know is you never told us about Times Square."

"I am never going to live this down, am I?" he asks.

"Not as long as you live," I smile. "And even if you didn't plan it, we're going to tell everybody you did."

Because time on the water is always too short, we usually try to squeeze far too much into each day of a trip. So after dinner, and despite an approaching storm, Young Tom hustles us off to the Lehigh River. Although the Lehigh is beautiful, I am now in a small stream state of mind and drift back to lower Hayes Run. Under dark thundering skies, I catch several more small brookies and then head for the car, where I find a tired Old Tom.

"My wife thinks I am out here having fun," he says.

His remark makes me appreciate my own weariness. We smile at each other, then Old Tom wanders over to the bridge across Hayes Run. I remove my vest and waders and join him to watch the water.

"This is what it's all about," he says after a moment. "Good fishing. Good friends. Good food." Almost as soon as the words are out of his mouth, the skies burst open, sending us hurrying for the car.

All that night the rain continues, plunging the temperature from the upper seventies to the low fifties. In the morning, Old Tom reiterates his long-standing belief that weather fronts affect the lateral line of trout and puts them down, making it useless to fish, but we are on the first trip of the season and on new water. Moments after breakfast, we rush out the door. We come to agree with Tom, though, when a couple hours of pounding Hayes Run produces only two tiny brookies.

When the front finally passes, Hickory Run adds credence to Old Tom's theory by turning friendly. I catch four brookies with my first dozen casts and then settle in to battle a fifth fish rising under an overhanging rhododendron. The contest ends when the trout darts out to grab my Light Cahill off what I had thought was a bad cast. I move on to find Old Tom standing over a deep shaded pool, line wrapped around the end of his rod and a stunned expression on his face.

"You wouldn't believe the fish I just missed," he says. "He had to be every bit of twenty inches. I never expected him."

Offering my condolences, I find a sunny spot and sit down on a log jutting out of a brush pile. The morning is chillier than we had expected and the sun feels good. There is nothing so warm as the May sun. Like robins and the smell of lilacs, it is one of the finest aspects of spring.

Watching Tom cast into the eddy alongside the rock, I think he is wasting his time. Twenty-inch trout do not strike a second time or they would never have grown to be twenty-inch trout, but I understand what he is doing, trying to will the fish back. I have done it many times myself. Quietly, I sit watching him and enjoying the sun, until it feels like time for a beer. Stiff from two days of casting, I push myself up off the log and, suddenly, jump back, startled by an unexpected movement at my feet. Snake!

Once I regain my composure, I see that the snake has stopped only a few feet away on a sunny rock. The sun feels as good to him as it does to me, and he does not want to give it up. Curious about the species, I move closer until a slit eye and a triangular head tell me it's a copperhead.

Anybody who fishes has at one time or another been warned about snakes, usually rattlesnakes. Some anglers are so paranoid when it comes to snakes, they won't go near waters where they have been told there are snakes, which is one sure way to keep a stream from becoming overcrowded. But the chances of being bitten by a poisonous snake in Pennsylvania are so slim as to be nearly nonexistent. Far more people hit the lottery and become millionaires each year than are bitten by snakes.

Even seeing a poisonous snake in Pennsylvania is becoming rarer all the time. In almost four decades as a fisherman, I have yet to encounter a rattlesnake in the woods and can remember just three or four copperheads. Bill Allen, author of *The Snakes of Pennsylvania* and retired supervisor of reptiles and amphibians at the Pittsburgh Zoo, says Pennsylvania has lost so much snake habitat that he has to search an entire day to find three or four copperheads or rattlesnakes in places where thirty years ago he would have found twenty or thirty. Even when encountered head-on, chances are good that a poisonous snake will either be passive or flee. Rattlesnakes and copperheads are not belligerent or aggressive creatures. They don't chase people and often cannot even be provoked into striking. "I've stepped on them and never had them bite," Allen told me. "I've photographed them and tried to get them to bite my boot, and I'd have to take ten pictures before I could even get them to put their fangs out."

When a rattlesnake or copperhead does strike, there is a 30 percent chance it will be a "dry bite" in which no venom is injected. Bill serves as a consultant on snake bites for several hospitals in the Pittsburgh area and says that, over the past ten years, he has been called in on bites only about a dozen times—a minuscule number considering the roughly three million people who live in the metropolitan area and the tens of millions of days they spend outdoors annually. Roger Latham, the late *Pittsburgh Press* outdoors writer, perhaps said it best when he wrote: "If you see one rattlesnake in your lifetime be thankful and enjoy it."

By the time we reach White Haven and the Lehigh in the evening, the sky is a cloudless blue and there is a new softness to the light. It is the light of approaching summer, with shadows that speak of warmth instead of cold. Time is running away, I think. Tomorrow we leave for home and a feeling of melancholy drifts through me.

In White Haven, we park in the cinder lot of an abandoned brick building that once belonged to either a coal company or a railroad. Young Tom leads us into the woods where he soon loses the path, launching a storm of jokes about his sense of direction and reminders of Times Square. The jokes only increase when we pass two parking lots closer to the river.

Eventually, we emerge from the woods at the downstream end of an island covered with burnt black stubble. It is separated from the bank by a narrow channel. After crossing the channel we scatter, and I find a spot above the riffle running off the tail of the island. For a half hour, I work the riffle with big nymphs and streamers without moving a fish, then decide to try the flats upstream. When they, too, are uncooperative, I decide to wait out the river.

Walking up the bank, I notice a few swallows winging back and forth over the water and think "Hatch." When I stop to stare at the air, though, no insects are visible. Whatever the swallows are feeding on must be sporadic and small. I watch the water for rising fish but see nothing.

"Do any good?" I ask Jack when I reach him.

"Nah," he answers. "But there are some Sulphurs and Cahills starting to come off. Shouldn't be long."

Since nothing is happening on the surface, I tie on a Hare's Ear nymph and on the second drift hook a fish. The battle lasts all of three seconds, but it is enough to start the juices flowing. My casting gains intensity. Then there are more flies in the air. The Sulphurs and Cahills are joined by caddis flies, Gray Fox, and what appear to be March Browns. Soon the air over the water is filled with light-colored insects, they look like apple blossoms blowing in a storm; but rises remain almost nonexistent.

Finally, Young Tom hooks a couple of fish near the head of the riffle, and Jack takes a nice brown of about fourteen inches. The catches are nothing, though,compared to the amount of flies on the water. Bugs are everywhere. It is far from the first time I've seen a river covered with flies and no fish rising, but it remains incomprehensible to me. A trout's life depends upon getting the most food for the least expenditure of energy. Those that survive are the opportunists prepared to grab whatever comes their way, yet the river is covered with food and we haven't seen a dozen rise forms. Such unpredictability may be interesting to contemplate and discuss back at camp, but on the water this is one of the worst forms of frustration life has to offer.

Thinking the fish may be feeding on emergers, I tie on an Olive Soft-Hackle and work the water in a series of long swings, one of which comes to a sudden stop. I lift my rod expecting the fish to make a run, but it comes straight toward me with only a shake of its head.

"It's a goddamn pike!" I shout when it finally comes into view. "I don't believe it!" The fish actually turns out to be a pickerel of about eighteen inches. My first pickerel on a fly.

"What a trip," I call to Jack, as he hurries over with his camera. "When are we coming back?"

Backlash

Although it would have been impossible for Pennsylvania's land and water to have been decimated without the consensus of the general population, not everybody agreed with the philosophy of endless consumption and the accumulation of extreme wealth. Not everybody stood by silently, either. In 1724, Pennsylvania enacted one of the first laws to deal with fishing in the New World when the colonial assembly passed a bill calling for the destruction of dams and weirs on the Schuylkill River. Even at that early date, so many fish-catching devices were in place on the Schuylkill that runs of shad had been depleted and navigation had become dangerous. Among the people who complained were relatives of Daniel Boone, who was born near Reading on November 2, 1734. On numerous occasions, the Boones struck dams while transporting wheat and had "to leap into ye River, and have very narrowly Escaped with their lives and Loads."

Enacting a law and enforcing it are two vastly different matters, however. Without wardens to make arrests, fishermen simply ignored that law, and similar ones passed in 1730 and 1734. The problem peaked on April 20, 1738, when frustrated farmers living above Valley Forge obtained an order from Justice of the Peace George Boone and—led by Timothy Miller and Constable William Richards—set out in a fleet of small craft to destroy the traps and dams, which brought out the fishermen to defend their property. Back and forth the battle raged, until Thomas Valentine, one of the fishermen, leaped into Miller's canoe and "struck out lustly upon all sides with a club, and after beating down every man of its crew succeeded in effecting its capture."

His thumb broken, Miller ordered a retreat. The farmers fled down the Schuylkill and then up Perkiomen Creek, which turned out to be a mistake. The stream was too shallow. The farmers were forced to abandon their boats and flee into the woods. The fishermen pursuing them destroyed the farmers' boats and "returned to their homes elated with a triumph which had been dearly purchased with many severe wounds and the loss of their racks."

Constable Richards, however, saw things differently. In a deposition given a week later, he stated that he had identified himself as a law officer and had informed the rack owners that he and the other men in his party had come to enforce the law. He had ordered them "in the Kings Name to Keep the Peace." The fishermen had "Damn'd the Laws & the Law-makers & Curs'd this Deponent & his Assistants" and attacked the party with clubs, leaving one of his deputies, John Wainwright, "Dead with his Body on the Shoar & his ffeet in the River." Public sentiment was so outraged by the attack upon the constable that the fishermen were forced to remove all fish dams and traps along the Schuylkill River.

Massachusetts enacted what may have been the first state law applying to fish in 1822, when it passed a bill proposed by Daniel Webster to protect trout and pickerel. Pennsylvania's first law specifically protecting fish was a local ordinance passed in 1829 that set a limit on trout in Big Spring, Cumberland County. Although the law—which forbade netting and limited fishing to the months between April and July—involved only a single stream, it gained wider attention when angling writer George Gibson referred to it in *American Turf Register and Sporting Magazine*. A scattering of municipalities across Pennsylvania enacted various ordinances governing fish and rivers beginning in the 1830s, but there would be no state agency to enforce fish laws until 1866. Pennsylvania would not have its first statewide law protecting trout until 1889.

Shad was such an important fish to early Pennsylvanians that it was the subject of the first case brought before the U.S. Supreme Court. Case No. 1 on the Supreme Court docket gave joint jurisdiction over shad runs in the lower Delaware River to Pennsylvania, New Jersey, and Delaware. In 1833, Pennsylvania and New Jersey clashed again over shad when the New Jersey legislature extended the shad season on the Delaware. Pennsylvanians living along the river reacted angrily, and a commission was formed to hear complaints and study the extended season's effect on the shad run. The commission concluded that shad should be protected, but its report was essentially ignored and matters went from bad to worse. By the end of the Civil War, dams, overfishing, and pollution seriously impeded or destroyed shad runs on the Delaware, as well as on the Schuylkill, Lehigh, and Susquehanna Rivers.

It was in reaction to the drastic decline of the state's shad fishery, as well as the "bad condition" of many mountain lakes and streams, that in early 1866, a convention of influential sportsmen from around Pennsylvania convened in Harrisburg. The convention drafted a law based on a law passed the previous year by Massachusetts. Act No. 336 provided for the appointment of a commissioner to investigate the shad problem on the Susquehanna. When it was signed by Governor Andrew Curtin on March 30, 1866, the Pennsylvania Fish Commission was created.

Act No. 336 called for the appointment of a single commissioner "who shall be a man of known probity and of experience, as a practical civil engineer." James Worrall of Harrisburg was chosen to fill the post, and his first action was to inform the Tide Water Canal Company that it would have to open a fish passage in its dam at Columbia on the Susquehanna River. The Tide Water Canal Company willingly complied with the order. Other companies with dams resisted the new law, however. They claimed they had purchased their dams from the state free of encumbrances and that Worrall's demand for fish passages was an unconstitutional infringement upon their property rights. Worrall countered by filing suit, thus launching a bitter four-year-long legal battle, which ended only when the Pennsylvania supreme court ruled that the companies involved were not compelled to make openings in the dams at their own expense.

Blocked from reaching their spawning grounds, shad held steady for two seasons after the passage was added to the Tide Water Dam, and then their numbers rapidly declined. Catches above the dam dropped from between 15,000 and 20,000 fish in 1867 to less than 5,000 in 1869. Poor design made it difficult for shad to make it through the passage in the Tide Water Dam and resulted in thousands of fish piling up below the dam, where their presence unleashed a feeding frenzy. People living along the river used "every device, however unfair, which came to their way to catch shad." So merciless was the slaughter that the general assembly in 1868 passed a law making it illegal to fish with a net or trap within two hundred yards of a dam with a fish passage. Once again the law was ignored.

Despite such failures, the legislature felt there were enough elements of success in the fight to continue efforts to save Pennsylvania's fisheries. On April 29, 1873, the Fish Commission was enlarged from one to three members, its powers were increased, and funds were provided to cover some expenses. The first three commissioners appointed under the act were Howard I. Reeder, Benjamin L. Hewit, and James Duffy.

Turning once again to the Susquehanna, which was considered to be in better condition than the Delaware and so more amenable to conservation efforts, the enlarged commission undertook a study to determine the causes for deterioration of shad runs in the lower river. The study pointed to drift net fishing, a too short and generally ignored closed season, and fish baskets injuring the young of the year.

Backed by the study, the commissioners set out to remove all fish baskets from the Susquehanna, but they immediately ran into problems. The law governing fish baskets required that county sheriffs give ten days' notice to basket owners before taking any action to remove the traps. Consequently, basket owners would wait until a day or two before the deadline and then simply move the baskets to a new location. Since the law contained no penalty for using fish baskets, even if a basket owner was caught there was nothing the sheriff could do except destroy the apparatus, which the owner would rebuild as soon as the sheriff was out of sight.

Drift net fishing was a large and powerful business with too much political support to simply outlaw it, so the Fish Commission countered by seeking a longer closed period. In 1873 a law was passed that prohibited the setting of nets on Sundays. This was followed over the next several years by other laws that gave sheriffs the right to destroy fish baskets without prior notice, extended the Sunday closed period, and set a list of fines. But laws do not change attitudes, and the violations continued. A commission report noted: "The average fisherman thinks that his right is one of the original inalienable rights of the Declaration of Independence, the greatest indeed of them all, and he respects no statute that impedes his operations."

Although new laws and better enforcement proved critical ingredients in stemming the destruction of Pennsylvania's fisheries, by the beginning of the 1870s it was becoming clear that something would have to be done to replace the decimated fish populations. From New Yorker Seth Green, the father of American fish culture, the commission purchased the right to use his patented hatchery boxes for three years at a cost of $2,000.

Under the guidance of one of Green's assistants, the boxes were set up on the Susquehanna River in Perry County; 2.7 million shad were hatched and released into the river in 1873. Similar boxes erected along the river at Marietta and Columbia, Lancaster County, produced another 500,000 fish, pushing the total hatching of shad to 3.2 million for the first year of hatchery operations in Pennsylvania.

Realizing that a hatchery also was needed for cold-water species, the Fish Commission in 1873 started a trout and salmon propagation facility on Hoovers Spring at its junction with Donegal Spring Creek near Marietta. The commission then hired John Creveling, a protégé of Thaddeus Norris, as superintendent and launched a tradition of experimenting with foreign species that continues to this day. The first eggs placed in the troughs at Marietta belonged to Pacific salmon or, as they were then called, "California salmon." A shipment of 150,000 eggs was purchased from the U.S. Fish Commission but arrived in such bad shape that only about 1,000 hatched and were released into a forgotten tributary of the Susquehanna.

To make up for the loss of salmon, the commission purchased 100,000 brook trout eggs from the state of New York. Creveling himself traveled to Rochester to pick up the eggs and make sure they arrived in good condition. This time a large percentage of the eggs hatched, and the fry were stocked in streams in the western half of the state the following spring.

The Fish Commmission was aware that restocking Pennsylvania's mountain streams with trout was going to take an enormous effort. Feeling that its limited funds might better be spent on fish such as shad and bass, which lived in large rivers and were accessible to more people, the Fish Commission after its first attempt with brook trout decided to leave the restocking of trout to future generations. So that those generations might have something to work with, though, ponds were built on the ground of the Marietta Hatchery in which brood stocks of trout were kept.

The decision to forgo trout stocking is more understandable when the hardship of hatchery work in the 1870s is considered. Fish were generally transported in milk cans that held fifteen gallons of water. The heavy cans had to be moved by hand, and the water in them aerated by a worker with a dipper. Transporting the cans over the mountains was done on horse-drawn wagons along trails that were roads in name only. In the winter, hatchery men often had to abandon their beds to make sure the eggs did not freeze, and they underwent all these trials and tribulations for a public that often viewed them as nothing more than fish merchants, as is evident in a letter, one of many in the same vein, the commission received from a Philadelphia man in the 1890s: "Dear Sir: Please send me some of them trout fry I hear of as I am fond of fried trout."

Government, of course, could not do everything. Anglers also played an important role in restoring and replenishing Pennsylvania's rivers and streams. The Schuylkill Fishing Company in 1868 spent $158.96 to purchase 120 bass for stocking in the Schuylkill River. Thaddeus Norris followed suit two years later when he bought 450 bass, which he placed in the Delaware River. In 1903, citizens of Bellefonte, Centre County, raised $3,500, which they donated to the Fish Commission to purchase land for a hatchery. Two years later, residents of Crawford County made a gift to the state of Crawford Hatchery near Conneaut Lake.

Wealthy sportsmen also helped to preserve portions of the nation's landscape and wildlife through sporting clubs, which caused something of a conflict of interest, since many of the sportsmen's business affairs were at the same time destroying countless acres of forests and thousands of miles of streams throughout the country. The clubs purchased or leased vast tracts of land on which members could hunt, fish, and practice conservation techniques. Among the best known of these reserves was the Blooming Grove Association in Pike County.

The idea for Blooming Grove was originated in the late 1860s by Fayette Giles, a wealthy New York jeweler, and Genio Scott, author of *Fishing in American Waters,* one of the earliest guidebooks to fishing in North America. The two men saw that most of the good fishing and hunting opportunities remaining in the United States had moved west, out of reach of the businessmen in New York and other East Coast cities who could not afford to leave their businesses for weeks at a time to travel to the Rocky Mountains. What was needed, these two men decided, was a place where game and fish could be bred and protected, as in European game preserves, within a reasonable distance of New York. According to Charles Hallock, editor of *Forest & Stream* and a founding member of the club, Pike County was chosen because

> fine streams were found running through pleasant valleys,
> eight beautiful lakes were within easy walking distance of
> each other, and a range of high wooded hills crossed the
> southern end of the tract. To add to the advantages and
> attractions of the country, deer were already found in the
> woods in great numbers, and woodcock, ruffed-grouse and
> wild pigeons were met with at every turn. The streams
> were already stocked with splendid trout, and the tract
> seemed a sportsman's paradise.

Blooming Grove Park Association was incorporated in March 1871, and it purchased about twelve thousand acres in Blooming Grove, Porter, and Greene townships near where Promised Land State Park is now. Within three years, the club had about one hundred members dedicated to

> the importing, acclimating, propagating, and preserving of
> all game animals, fur-bearing animals, birds, and fishes
> adapted to the climate . . . the cultivation of forests; and the
> selling of timber and surplus game of all kinds; in a word,
> to give a fuller development to field, aquatic and turf
> sports, and to compensate in some degree for the frightful
> waste which is annually devastating our forests and exter-
> minating our game.

Blooming Grove set up game and fish regulations that were much more severe than anything enacted by the state. Poachers were fined $2 for every fish in their possession and $5 per the total poundage of fish. The fine for killing an elk or moose was $300 and for a deer $40. The club's gamekeepers were made deputy sheriffs and given arrest powers to enforce fines.

As often happens in cases where wealthy sportsmen take over an area, however, many people living in the vicinity of Blooming Grove did not like the club, even though, if it had not been for such clubs, there would have been even less fish and wildlife left in Pennsylvania—and other eastern states—by the dawn of the twentieth century. The Game Commission purchased white-tailed deer from these clubs to aid its restocking efforts, while the Fish Commission bought thousands of trout to supplement what was being produced in its own hatcheries. Blooming Grove and other clubs also served as examples for game and fish management programs and conservation laws. According to historian Theodore W. Cart,

> The concept and execution of the Blooming Grove plan provided the first large-scale demonstration of integrated natural resource planning for primarily recreational purposes in America, something that would not be approached in the public sector for twenty years. . . . Yellowstone Park, created in the next year [1872], had no effective game protection until 1894 and had no plan to cultivate its timber. . . . Blooming Grove had no public counterparts until the national forest system provided for multiple use of timber and game resources.

Since public funds were being expended to save fisheries, popular support was important. To gain this support, early conservationists often promoted their stocking efforts as ways to increase food supplies. For this reason, and because humans tend to think they can improve on nature, the Pennsylvania Fish Commission, the U.S. Fish Commission, sportsmen's clubs, and individuals all undertook a variety of exotic stocking projects in the late nineteenth century. Among the cold-water species experimented with were lake trout, Atlantic, Pacific, and landlocked salmon, rainbow trout, and brown trout.

Salmon were valuable food fish for thousands of years before William Penn suggested their presence in the upper Delaware

River. No evidence exists that the species ever occurred naturally in the river, but the almost universal opinion was that the Delaware was suitable for the fish. Consequently, in 1871 anglers from Philadelphia and Easton purchased 10,000 Atlantic salmon eggs from the Canadian government. The eggs were hatched in Duchess County, New York, and the fry taken to Easton in late May. Hot weather immediately claimed all but about 2,500 of the fry. The survivors were placed in a spring on Bushkill Creek above Easton, and two other nearby springs.

The following year, more eggs were brought to the Delaware. According to the Fish Commission report for 1892: "Mr. Thaddeus Norris took charge of these himself and undertook to have them hatched under his own supervision at a spring about a mile from Easton. Notwithstanding the hatching boxes were of the rudest description, Mr. Norris succeeded in successfully incubating 11,000. These were also placed in a tributary of the Delaware."

Taking note of such efforts, the U.S. Fish Commission in 1873 gave Pennsylvania and New Jersey each 40,000 Atlantic salmon spawn from Maine's Kennebec River. Approximately 60,000 of the eggs were hatched and most of them released into tributaries of the Delaware.

About the same time, the Fish Commission also sought to introduce Pacific salmon into the Susquehanna River. Today, the idea of stocking a cold-water species like salmon in a river as warm and shallow as the Susquehanna seems absurd. Fish culturists in the 1870s, however, saw the Susquehanna as similar to rivers in California from which they obtained salmon spawn. Nobody bothered to compare water temperatures. In the spring of 1873 about 6,000 Pacific salmon were placed in the river near Harrisburg and that fall another 21,000 were released into tributaries of the Susquehanna. Although doomed from the start, the stockings in the Susquehanna and Delaware produced a great deal of excitement among fishermen and some interesting catches. "In 1877 much excitement was caused by the capture of a large salmon thirty-two inches long in Givetzinger's mill race on the Bushkill," the Fish Commission's 1892 report notes.

In the same year a number of others were taken in the Delaware, and one "fine specimen," presumably a Pacific salmon, in the Susquehanna. Between that date and 1879 several other specimens were captured in the Delaware river, some of them weighing as much as twenty-five pounds, and on May 11, 1879, a female, measuring three feet four and a half inches, and weighing about seventeen pounds, was captured in a gill net off Spesuter Island in the Susquehanna river.

Salmon catches in both the Delaware and the Susquehanna Rivers ceased after 1879, and in 1884 the Fish Commission abandoned the program. Warm-water species stocked in Pennsylvania during the late nineteenth century included striped bass, walleye, crappie, rock bass, white perch, yellow perch, black bass, and (one of the greatest mistakes in the history of fish management, perhaps the best evidence of what can happen when humans decide they can improve on nature) the carp.

A native of Asia, carp were cultivated as a food fish in Austria as early as 1227. Germany and Poland had the fish by the fourteenth century and England by the start of the sixteenth century. In Europe, though, the carp was generally treated as a domestic creature and, like sheep or pigs, raised in enclosures. The two men most responsible for the carp's spread across the Atlantic were Rudolph Hessel and Spencer Baird. Hessel was a biologist who published a study of the carp in the 1870s, in which he concluded "there is no other fish which will, with proper management, be advantageous as the carp."

Hessel provided the scientific support, but it was Baird who actually must bear the blame for introducing the carp to America. As head of the U.S. Fish Commission, he imported carp eggs into the country in 1877 and, for several years afterward, shipped millions of them to practically anybody who wanted them. "I have great faith in the future of this new fish," he wrote in 1880, "and am quite well satisfied that within ten years it will constitute a very prominent element in the food animals of the country."

That same year, members of the Pennsylvania Fish Commission determined that carp probably would flourish in the Susquehanna and Juniata Rivers and Commissioner Hewit gave three fry to James McCahan, who lived near Holidaysburg, Blair County, for planting in a pond. Two of the fish (one died in the pond) were removed from McCahan's impoundment in July 1880 and released into the Frankstown Branch Juniata River. "The temperature of the water there being cool, as compared to the lower waters of the Juniata and Susquehanna," the commission's 1879 report concludes, "we can hope for the most gratifying results in open streams in the introduction of this most prolific and valuable fish."

By the early 1890s, however, the commission was whistling another tune. Americans did not like the carp in any way, shape, or form. The commission's 1894 report states:

> Utterly ignoring whatever merits there may be attached to the carp, it is quite certain that the majority of anglers are more apt to execrate the man who first introduced the fish quite heartily as they might Benedict Arnold, or the misguided men who originally imported the English sparrow. In fact, there are few fishes more heartily anathemized by American anglers. They fail to see a single redeeming feature in the creature, and charge it with many bad qualities, the most serious among which is the allegation that it is a more inveterate spawn eater than the eel. The fecundity of the fish is so great that it is overrunning all the rivers and streams of the country.

The Fish Commission abandoned its carp cultivation program in 1895. By then, of course, it was far too late.

The fight to preserve Pennsylvania's fisheries also led to some unusual turns involving the law. Among these was what might be called "The Case of the Landing Net," or "When Is a Fish Caught?"—one of the most unusual court fights in fish and game law history. It began in April 1898, when John Ely, William Seiple, and Joseph Delp of Northampton County went fishing in a stretch of McMichaels Creek, Monroe County, that was controlled by the Pohoqualine Fish Association, whose membership was made up of well-to-do sportsmen from Philadelphia. These three decided to fish the creek because a recent ruling by the state supreme court seemed to make it legal to fish in any stream in which the Fish Commission ever stocked fish.

According to witnesses for the club, Ely, Seiple, and Delp ignored sixty-three printed notices declaring the water private and left only after two fish wardens appeared and threw rocks in the water around the men to prevent them from catching fish. Returning in the afternoon, the men "endeavored to bribe the wardens who were persistent in their efforts to prevent their fishing." The bribe attempt resulted in the men being cited for trespass, and at the trial that followed they were found guilty and fined one dollar each.

In retaliation, sympathizers of Ely, Seiple, and Delp countered a year later by causing the arrest of William Elliot and J. Price Wetherill, officers of the Pohoqualine club, on a charge of using a net to catch fish in McMichaels Creek in violation of state law. The net in question was a landing net and the issue before the court was whether the trout actually had been caught with a landing net or by the defendant's hook.

Common sense might say the fish had been caught with a rod using a line and a hook, but common sense in the courtroom often falls victim to an attorney's choice of words and facts. Wetherill and Elliot were found guilty and fined $100 each. The decision led to an appeal and a debate as to exactly when a fish is considered "caught." As fishermen are probably the only people equal to lawyers when it comes to semantics, the court case also led to some amusing testimony, including the following exchange, which began when a witness testified that fishermen "could not save as many fish without the landing net as with it."

"What do you mean by *save*?" asked the defense attorney.

"I mean to put them in a basket. When they are tied up tight then they are saved. That is what I mean by *saving fish*."

"What do you mean by *catch*?"

"I mean when they strike the hook, get firmly caught by the hook."

"What do you mean by *catch*?" the attorney asked again.

"When I catch a fish it is when the fish strikes the fly, hooks himself, then he is caught. He sometimes gets away."

"*Catch* and *caught* are only different tenses of the same word," the attorney pointed out. "Don't you know the dictionary definition of the word *catch*?"

"Well, perhaps you better read it to me," the fisherman responded.

The defense attorney then asked the judge for his definition of the word *catch*, to which the judge replied: "It means when the fish strikes the fly and hooks himself. Then he is caught and that means to catch a fish with the hook, then the hook catches him."

Returning to the witness, the defense attorney asked: "If you are fishing with a fly and you hook a fish do you consider him caught?"

"I do, sir," the angler replied, "until he gets away."

"If you have been fishing and on your return home, you are asked how many fish you caught, do you count those that were on the hook, or those in your basket?"

"I sometimes count them both ways."

"Do you consider the fish caught then before it is taken from its element?"

"Yes, sir; most unquestionably."

Attempting a different tack, the defense attorney noted that state laws prohibited the "catching of fish" under a certain size and required that any one catching fish under that size return them to the water. Then he asked the fisherman/witness: "Now what did the legislature mean by *catching*? Did they mean that the fish should actually be in the possession of the party?"

"I give it up," was all the fisherman would say.

After listening to several more such witnesses, a thoroughly confused judge could only rule: "A trout may be said to be caught when held by a hold, as well as when in the landing net or creel."

Thus, some of Pennsylvania's finest legal minds were stumped when it came to determining exactly when a fish is caught. They had to settle on three possible instances. The judges did rule, however, that the law prohibiting the use of nets to catch fish did not apply to landing nets. Mistakes such as the stocking of carp and absurdities such as the landing net case aside, if it were not for the farsighted efforts of many now-forgotten individuals, fishing in Pennsylvania might have been totally destroyed. These efforts serve as proof that a handful of dedicated conservationists can make a difference.

Drought Warnings

Since I had broken the rules, I normally would not have been happier. Few things in life give me more pleasure than bucking the tide and succeeding; even when that success is so inconsequential as taking brown trout on a cloudless afternoon from shallow, placid, glass-clear water. But after five days of fishing, there is little joy or excitement left even when I catch and release two eighteen-inchers in less than twenty minutes. The water seems to be getting lower by the hour. Neither of the fish puts up much of a fight and I feel guilty adding to their woes for my pleasure. Quietly, I snip off the beetle that has worked so well, hook it into the fleece patch on my vest, reel in my line, and head back to the cabin.

The word from Potter County before we left Pittsburgh was mixed. Kettle Creek was full of fish and hatches were good. Coffin Flies, Sulphurs, and Gray Foxes were on the water. Walt Siegfried and Norm Hummon, two friends from the Pittsburgh Fly Fishers, had taken 305 trout during their annual week at Cross Fork. Walt lost one close to six pounds and caught six others over eighteen inches, I was told. The problem was the water. When they arrived it had been clear, and a pleasant sixty degrees. Damn near perfect. By the end of the week, though, stretches of stream that were normally ten inches deep in early June had dropped to trickles and the fish had retreated to a few deep holes.

After the drought of two years ago, news of low water has everybody worried. At the same time it is tough to believe it could happen again, after all the rain of April and May. Looking at Kettle Creek, however, it appears as if all the warnings have been correct. The rain of last year was enough only to refill the state's reservoirs; still more is needed to replenish the groundwater. Last month's downpours have not helped. Most of that water ran off before it could be absorbed into the ground to replenish the water table. Droughts, of course, are nothing new. They are part of the natural weather cycle, but something about having two in three years, especially following the wettest summer in more than a century, seems abnormal. Global warming?

Recently, I've been reading stories claiming that global warming is a fallacy. Some right-wing polemicists even suggest the theory might be a plot to weaken America. They use the word *environmentalist* the same way they once used *communist* and refer contemptuously to anybody who wants to rein in development and save something for the future as "greenies." They claim everything is fine, there is nothing to worry about, but they never present much evidence to support their claim and they conveniently ignore, or use only selectively, the mass of data on the subject. Instead of a mere statistical blip, three cool rainy days in the middle of summer become proof that global warming is a fraud.

I remember a guest editorial in the *Pittsburgh Post-Gazette*, which claimed that "the historical record shows a sharp increase in carbon dioxide is nothing short of bogus." It drew a number of responses. Among the most reasonable was one from Bruce Hapke, a faculty member in the University of Pittsburgh's Department of Geology and Planetary Science. After pointing out that data collected from many sources have determined that the abundance of carbon dioxide in the atmosphere has increased by about 33 percent since 1850, Hapke wrote: "The time period in which the increased carbon-dioxide concentration occurred coincides with the industrial revolution, but because there are natural sources of the gas it cannot be positively shown that industrial carbon dioxide is the cause. The cycle of carbon dioxide through the atmosphere, biosphere, oceans and crust of the earth is not well understood." Hapke noted that scientists cannot agree if the rise in carbon dioxide has been accompanied by an increased mean annual temperature because of naturally occurring, random fluctuations in temperatures. However, he said: "Mean temperatures over the past fifteen years have been the highest since record-keeping began, and there also has been a worldwide decrease in the sizes of glaciers over the past century."

Given the lack of firm conclusions, Hapke suggests two courses of action. One is to do nothing and bet that predictions of catastrophe are the work of "environmental wackos." The second is to assume that global warming may occur and take steps to neutralize it by reducing emissions from factories and power stations, stepping up research on alternative power sources, and encouraging Detroit to develop competitive cars powered by fuel cells or other alternative propulsion systems. "The advantage of the second option is that it may prevent a global catastrophe," Hapke concluded. "The disadvantage is that it might prove to have been unnecessary. However, even if global warming is not imminent, the result would be cleaner and quieter cities and highways and a more pleasant planet. In that case, have we really wasted anything?"

With a slowly strangling Kettle Creek shining in the sun, I try to imagine life without trout. I shiver at the thought. Then memories of Potter County rush in. I cannot say exactly when I first heard of Potter County. Probably, it was from the deer kill reports in *Pennsylvania Game News*. Every year throughout my boyhood, Potter County was the number one county in the state for deer kills. Desperately wanting to prove myself a hunter, I imagined the county as my best chance to take a buck. I often dreamed of hunting its mountains, but my dad knew Warren County, so that was where my deer hunting career began.

My first opportunity to visit Potter County didn't come until I was out of college. Friends came back from a trip talking about rattlesnake hunts, wood-chopping contests, and deer "runnin' around like rabbits." They wore T-shirts and carried travel mugs urging "Do Your Sportin' in Wharton" and told tales about seven-foot-tall Indians with horns, and the Frenchman who lost his head and still roams the woods around Hammersley Fork. That was more than twenty-five years ago.

As often happened in those days, my first trip to Potter County involved more partying than fishing. We fished every day—Kettle Creek, the First Fork and East Fork of Sinnemahoning Creek—

but much more of the trip was given to simply exploring the country, drinking, smoking an occasional joint, and celebrating Christmas in July at the Cross Fork Inn. Christmas in July was so much fun, we made it a tradition for several years, which led to a number of other adventures, including one with the U.S. Army Special Forces, the Green Berets.

Tug was the first to encounter the troops. It happened one afternoon when he was on Kettle Creek. Suddenly, the sky filled with parachutes and he found himself surrounded by a dozen heavily armed men dressed in camouflage. Potter County being a place to escape, he worried for a moment that the old Cold War had turned hot and he'd missed it. Then he realized that money deducted from his paycheck had purchased the weapons the troops were toting and was relieved to find he wasn't about to be marched off to Siberia.

The next couple of days we seemed to run into the troops everywhere, especially in the bars. We got used to the sight and soon paid very little attention to them. Then one night Tug, Carby (a boyhood friend), and I were fishing at the Route 144 bridge over Kettle Creek. When it came time to leave, Tug and Carby took a short cut under the bridge to our vehicles. I couldn't resist another cast, which turned into twenty more minutes of fishing, until I broke off my fly and decided it would be more trouble than it was worth to tie on another in the darkness and gave up.

"Don't come under here," a voice quietly warned as I started under the bridge.

"What?" I asked puzzled.

"Don't come under here," the voice repeated.

"What the hell you mean don't come under here!" I asked, thinking I was talking to Tug.

"Stay out," the voice answered.

"Screw you," I said, and was about to walk under the bridge when a dark figure with a rifle stepped out in front of me.

"I've got it strung with booby traps," the shadow announced and sent me scrambling up the bank to where Tug and Carby stood laughing.

"We were hoping he'd shoot you," Tug said.

As the years passed, Potter County would help many of us survive broken marriages and romances, deaths of friends and family members, unemployment and relocation. In among those major trials its beauty, its isolation, and its trout always served well as an escape from stupid bosses, traffic jams, nosey neighbors, and business suits. Although we would continue to fish other areas, our focus shifted more and more to Kettle Creek and Cross Fork, "The Biggest Little Town in the World." Settling on a favorite stream is a complicated affair that involves more than mere numbers of fish. Kettle Creek evolved into our favorite Potter County stream because, along with fish, it also had good hatches then, a pine plantation where we could camp, and a couple of miles down the road, Cross Fork, Gabby Hayes, and Harry Kinney.

Since Cross Fork today consists essentially of a fire company, a couple of bars and four gas pumps, a tackle shop, and population of about eighty, our minds were totally boggled when we learned that Gabby Hayes—Roy Rodgers's sidekick in all those hokey 1940s cowboy movies—made his stage debut in Cross Fork. Our doubts were quickly dispelled when we entered Kinney's Bar and found an autographed picture of Gabby hanging on the wall. "I'll be darned" was the only appropriate response. Gabby had performed in Cross Fork near the start of the twentieth century when it was a lumber boomtown with three thousand permanent residents—and a like number of "wood hicks," as lumbermen were called, who frequently left the woods to partake of the town's fine assortment of brothels and gambling houses.

After Gabby first grabbed our attention, the man who held it until his death was Harry Kinney, the owner of the bar in which the picture of Gabby still hangs. None of us ever got to know Harry well; that was our fault, not his. Being young and hot for trout and partying, we seldom had time for talking on our trips to Cross Fork in those days, but like so many other pilgrims to Potter, we always felt we knew him because of his weekly column in the *Potter Leader-Enterprise*. It was the first thing we read in the paper. We loved hearing about his aches and pains, his wife ("The Boss"), his children, and the hunters and fishermen from the big cities, whom he always called "Lover Boys" and warned the local girls to watch out for. Through Harry's book *The Story of a Ghost Town*, we also learned the history of Cross Fork, a tale of boom and bust that was repeated time and again across the length and breadth of Pennsylvania. The name could just as well have been Slate Run, Rouseville, Saylorsville, Antes, Bendigo, Cedar Run, Tidioute, Tobyhanna, Leetonia, Gouldsboro, Pithole,

Galeton, Keating, Austin, Foxsburg, or Forksville.

For Cross Fork, it all began back in 1893, when southern Potter County was essentially a virgin wilderness, one so dense it was "impossible to read at midday" under the canopy. The darkness of the forest, coupled with what early settlers saw as a resemblance to Germany's famous forest, led the few hunters, trappers, and woodsmen who frequented the region to dub it the Black Forest. Then the Lackawanna Lumber Company arrived on the scene, and, driven by the lumber camp and sawmill that the lumber company built at the confluence of Cross Fork Creek and Kettle Creek, Cross Fork was the busiest town in Potter County by 1895. It contained five grocery stores, two clothing shops, a millinery, a dry goods shop, two drugstores, a hardware store, four churches, seven hotels, three doctors, two dentists, a wholesale liquor store, a YMCA, a Masonic Lodge, an Odd Fellows Hall, a newspaper, a school, along with water, electric, and sewage systems, a telephone company, and an opera house where Gabby Hayes made his debut in 1905.

Lackawanna Lumber's original sawmill was destroyed by a fire and was replaced with a larger mill in 1897, when the Pennsylvania Stave Company also set up operations in Cross Fork, making staves for wooden barrels and buckets. When Lackawanna's second mill also burned, the company built a third in 1903. This third mill had a daily production capacity of 230,000 board feet, which caused town residents to point out proudly that the mill's annual output was enough to circle the globe with boards an inch thick and twelve inches wide. Like countless other towns with economies dependent upon a limited resource or single industry, however, Cross Fork's days were numbered from the beginning.

The fatal blow came in April 1909, when Lackawanna Lumber closed its doors. For a time, the Pennsylvania Stave Company was able to slow the town's slide into oblivion by hiring Lackawanna workers, but the stave mill was too small to sustain Cross Fork for long. Then fire became a fact of life. So many homes and businesses went up in flames that insurance companies were hard pressed to cover losses. When an entire block burned in February 1910, insurers canceled all policies in Cross Fork. Just as suddenly as they began, the fires ended.

With no work and no possibility of collecting insurance

money, Cross Fork residents were forced to sell their homes for whatever the market would bear. Five-room houses with steam heat were offered for twenty-five dollars and seven-room homes for thirty-five dollars. But there were few takers. Owners began tearing down buildings and shipping everything salvageable to the next boomtown. In 1913, the Pennsylvania Stave Company closed its mill and the Buffalo & Susquehanna Railroad ended service to Cross Fork. By the time the United States entered World War I, Cross Fork's population had dwindled to sixty-one and all that remained was a hotel, three stores, and a school. The forests above town that had once brought darkness at noon were reduced to scrub brush, dotted by fire-blackened, rotting stumps of three-hundred- or four-hundred-year-old trees. Without vegetation to hold back the rains and shade their waters, Kettle Creek and Cross Fork Creek were choked with silt and sawdust, and empty of fish.

Sitting on the cabin porch, I find it tough to think that less than two weeks have passed since we left the near perfect waters of the Poconos. The trip has still been a good one, though. I saw my first bobcat. It was walking down Route 44 in the middle of the day. Despite its reputation as a shy, elusive creature, the animal was in no hurry to get off the road. When I stopped, it simply moved up the bank and lay down. We looked at each other for a good ten seconds. I could not take my eyes off its face. It was one of the most beautiful faces I've ever seen. No painting, sketch, or photograph could capture the essence of that wild feline grace. I wanted to follow it off into the woods.

Another afternoon on Cross Fork Creek, I brought up fifty-eight wild fish. None of them was over ten inches, but the one I hooked at a pool where two currents converged alone was worth it all. I knew at first sight the spot held a fish. He smashed my Royal Coachman the instant it touched the water. I lost him in a tangle of roots, but this was only a little disappointing. I had been right. Then, when I stepped out of the water into the high grass of a nearby island, I jumped a fawn that stopped only about ten feet away and gave me a good look.

Another evening, I was left openmouthed and hopeful of old age. It happened when I was wandering Kettle Creek looking for my friend Jack Hess. I found him with Bob Runk, founder of the Pittsburgh Fly Fishers. They were working a small pool protected by a pair of birch trees and not doing well at all.

"In fifty-four years of coming up here this is the worst I've ever seen it during the first week of June," Bob told me. "It's a crying shame."

Still, he continued to cast to the holding water under an overhanging birch until a trout rose and took his fly. Saddened by the fish's weak fight, he then announced he was calling it quits. Instead of taking the path along the low bank, though, he crossed the stream and, at age seventy-six, scrambled up the fifteen-foot-high bank like a gazelle.

Pioneers with Vice and Plane

At the same time Pennsylvania's original fisheries were being decimated, anglers with state ties were making important contributions to the advancement of sport fishing. Some of these pioneers' stories are well known, some are confused or shrouded in legend and misconception, others are essentially unknown. The stories start with rod pioneer Samuel Phillippe, developer of the modern six-strip split-cane rod.

Phillippe was born in Reading, Berks County, on August 1, 1801. He moved to Easton on the Delaware River, Northampton County, when he was sixteen years old. In Easton, he learned the trade of gunsmithing from Peter Young. Along with making guns and cane fishing rods, he also was skilled at making violins. One of his violins was awarded a silver medal by the Franklin Institute in Philadelphia.

According to a letter written by his son Solon, Phillippe also made fishing hooks from a pattern developed by Phineus Kinsey of Easton, and he fished with Thaddeus Norris. "He visited a number of places with Mr. Thad Norris, when the latter was seeking a location for a trout hatchery, and which was finally located near Bloomsburg, N.J.," Solon wrote. "Mr. Norris often saw Phillippe at work on split-bamboo rods in his shop."

Most of the evidence that Phillippe was the inventor of the six-strip split-cane rod comes from James Henshall's *Book of the*

Black Bass. Henshall reported in the first edition of his work in 1881 that Phillippe made his original rod in 1848, but after further research in later editions he revised that date backward to 1845, a date that is supported by several letters from friends and acquaintances of Phillippe, as well as rod companies with whom he did business. According to Solon Phillippe, his father sold his first rod in 1848: "This was a four-section rod in three pieces, all split-bamboo, including the butt."

Phillippe's original rods, according to Solon, had three sections. The butt was made of ash, the middle section and the tip were made of first two strips and then three strips of split cane. Phillippe soon found, though, that such two-strip and three-strip rods "would not cast the fly true," so he changed the design to four strips "and found that they would cast perfectly in any direction." He followed up the ash-and-cane design with rods made completely of four-strip cane and then with what Martin Keane, author of *Classic Rods and Rodmakers,* calls "truly a historic milestone for fishermen the world over"—the six-strip cane rod.

The British actually were making rods similar to Phillippe's two-strip and three-strip cane-and-ash creations as early as 1801. Keane writes that, "rods containing three- or four-strip bamboo sections were in fairly common use during the 1840s in England" and development of fishing rods was a wholly European effort until the 1840s. Whether Phillippe knew of the English rods is impossible to say. Henshall feels it is unlikely that an obscure gunmaker living in a small Pennsylvania town would have known of the rods, but it is possible Philadelphia or New York anglers traveling through Easton could have shown him a rod.

Those early British rods were made with the "enamel," the hard, shiny surface of the cane, both on the outside and on the inside of the rod. All of Phillippe's rods were made with the enamel on the outside. Rods made with the enamel on the outside kept water from seeping into the cane, making them more durable and longer-lasting than rods with the enamel on the inside.

One of the letter writers Henshall cites as proof that Phillippe developed the first six-strip cane rod calls the rod maker's first rods "poor things now." Henshall disputes this assessment. Judging from a Phillippe rod that he owned, Henshall writes that "Old Sam Phillippe knew just what a trout fly rod should be in its action, both in casting a fly and in playing a trout; and it is on these qualities of a rod that its merits should be judged, rather than the style of its construction or fine appearance."

Samuel Phillippe died in Easton on May 25, 1877. His son Solon, to whom he taught the trade, had made his first rod in 1859. He continued in the family business of gunsmithing and rod making after his father's death.

At the same time Samuel and Solon Phillippe were making rods in Easton, Elizabeth Benjamin was undertaking some of the first recorded efforts at identifying aquatic insects and imitating them with artificial flies. Benjamin annually spent the summer with her children and husband, a conductor on the Elmira, Williamsport & Northern Railroad, at Ralston, on Lycoming Creek in Lycoming County. A never-before-published 1934 letter by her son Joseph describes the region around Ralston and his mother's work:

> About 1858 and 1860 it [Lycoming Creek] became known as one of the best places for catching large speckled brook trout in that section of the state, parties would come to Ralston, from the big cities loaded down with all kind of fancy fishing tackle, but usually returned home with empty baskets, one day my mother noticed a man by the name of Conley who kept the only tavern in the place would go fishing every afternoon about sun-down a short distance from our house, and always returned with a mess of trout that would make every one set up and take notice.
>
> My mother got so interested in Mr. Conley's success she waded out in the creek unnoticed by Conley, and observed that the largest trout would always jump for certain kinds of flys when lighting on the water, believing she could imitate the kind of flys trout were taking, she mentioned it to my father, and they worked nights making nets; and would wade out in the creek and catch the flys [and] place them under glasses on a table until they would "shed their coats."
>
> In order to make the imitation flys to resemble the genuine ones, it was my job to procure certain kinds of fe[a]thers obtained from roosters, chickens, ducks, pigeons and bird nests, the feathers were shaped by my mother; fastened by hand to fish-hooks with different colored silk

thread; many tourists coming to Ralston soon found out the flys they had was not especially adapted to that locality for good trout fishing, and when they learned of the success of others who had purchased my mothers hand made flys, they paid her fabulous prices for all she could make.

Before her marriage, Benjamin had worked as a school teacher in Rochester, New York. Her son writes that she "was educated, of strong personality, high mental powers, and natural endowment for invention of practical and useful things." She died on June 13, 1908.

Along with the inventor of the first modern cane rod, Pennsylvania also gave birth to one of the most innovative and influential rod makers of the late nineteenth and early twentieth centuries, the relatively unknown Hiram Hawes: "I saw a 7 1/2-foot, 2 1/2 ounce Hawes two years ago and it overwhelmed me," wrote Harmon Henkin in *Fly Tackle: A Guide to the Tools of the Trade*. "It was . . . a magnificent instrument—deep mahogany brown, with Payne-like fittings colored dark blue and golden windings with brown tips. And the action? It started at the butt swell and moved slowly to the middle, where it picked up a basic rhythm with a No. 4 line that could pace my heart. Utterly erotic! I would consider dumping most of my rods for that dainty Hawes."

The birth of Hiram Webster Hawes in Honesdale, Wayne County, in 1857 marked the joining of two distinguished American crafts families of the period. His father, Dwight H. Hawes, was a member of a well-known local gunsmith family and his mother, Ann Leonard, a member of a renowned oar-making family. More important from an angling point of view, Hawes's mother was the sister of America's most important early cane rod maker, Hiram Leonard.

Since Easton and Honesdale lay along the routes sportsmen from New York and Philadelphia traveled to the fishing and hunting grounds of northeastern Pennsylvania, it also is possible that Hawes may have been exposed to the work of Phillippe. "It does seem plausible," Keane notes, "particularly considering the personal pride a sportsman gets when showing a fellow sportsman his new custom-built rod or firearm."

Keane adds further support to his opinion by noting that, after the Civil War, Honesdale was a center for first-quality native ash, material that Phillippe needed for his rod butts. The Leonard oar-making shop would have been a logical place for Phillippe to stop and inquire about, or even purchase, supplies of ash. Phillippe being a gunsmith, it would have been natural for him to know other gunsmiths in northeastern Pennsylvania. Although the exposure of Hawes to Phillippe is a matter of conjecture, there is no doubt about his relationship with his uncle, Hiram Leonard. It would seem he was even named after the great rod maker.

Born in Sebec, Maine, in 1831, Hiram Leonard had moved with his family to Honesdale in 1840 to be near a fresh supply of ash for their oars. Hiram's father, Lewis, died shortly after the family's move to Pennsylvania and the young Hiram's formal education ended at age fifteen. After leaving school, he taught himself engineering, and he did such a good job that he was hired by the Pennsylvania Coal Company and given the job of surveying mountains for new mine shafts. Leonard worked for the mining company until the coal dust, gas, and smoke he was constantly breathing made him seriously ill. He moved to Bangor, Maine, to recuperate, where he was joined in 1869 by his nephew, Hiram Hawes.

Ernest Schwiebert in *Trout* says it was Hawes's brother Loman who was the real mechanical genius of the family and who conceived the idea for the first beveler capable of cutting consistently uniform and precise bamboo strips for rods. Keane, however, says it was Leonard and Hawes, working in the evenings and in their spare time, who invented the beveler. Keane credits Loman with developing the Leonard ferrule.

Whatever the truth or degree of truth in either theory, since the three men worked together and each one could have contributed something to the beveler's design, both authors, as well as other writers on the subject, agree that the Leonard beveler was a work of genius. Schwiebert says it "still remains one of the finest ever designed," while Keane maintains that its invention was "a task that even today would strain the thinking of a great many engineering minds." Keane goes on to conclude that the mathematical formulas and tapers used with the beveler are the foundation from which "virtually all the world's early sophisticated split-bamboo rods evolved."

Away from the shop, Hawes earned a reputation as one of the nation's best fly casters. He won dozens of awards from the 1880s through the early 1900s. In 1898, he married Leonard's daughter, his cousin Cora, who that same year became the first woman ever to win a national fly-casting championship.

Loman Hawes, along with Fred Thomas and E. W. Edwards, left the Leonard shop in 1898 and formed the rod-making firm of Thomas, Edwards & Hawes. Loman soon sold his interest in the company to Edward Payne and died suddenly sometime around the start of the twentieth century. Hiram Hawes stayed with the Leonard company until two years after his uncle's death in 1907. Then he moved his family (including his mother-in-law, Leonard's widow, Elizabeth) to Canterbury, Connecticut, where he began manufacturing his own line of rods.

Family problems reportedly kept Hawes from producing rods at a consistent level after he formed his own company. "This hypothesis is given some credibility," Henkin notes, "by apologetic notes in the 1917 and 1921 Abercrombie & Fitch catalogs for 'long delays' in receiving Hawes rods." H. W. Hawes & Company made fewer than 1,000 rods, 315 of which were actually made by Hawes's son Merritt, which makes them among the rarest finds on the antique rod market today. Hiram Hawes died on December 14, 1929.

PART 4

Dog Days

Dancing Fish

At the same time all fishing trips are good, they also are bad. They are bad for one reason. They end. They end and we have to leave life as we feel it should be and return to jobs we hate, unpaid bills, deadlines, mates we never should have married, children who think we are the stupidest creatures on earth, loneliness, and all those other things that add up to the lives of quiet desperation Thoreau saw all around him. Once, when I was working for somebody I loathed in a job that bored me to tears and I came back from a two-week trip to Montana, where I had been sleeping on the banks of the Madison and Yellowstone Rivers, I became so depressed I stopped talking, went into a stupor, and nearly sent my home life down the drain.

Under normal circumstances, I can usually count on a certain mellowness to hold onto through the first day home following a fishing trip. But after Potter, everything goes downhill immediately, beginning as soon as I walk into my apartment and see the mess I left behind. In the corner are stacks of boxes that need to be unpacked. Leaning against the bookcases are photographs and posters that need to be hung. On the shelves my books are out of order. The floor around the couch is littered with newspapers. My kitchen table and desk are so heavily laden with magazines and assorted papers, I can see wood only at one corner. The apartment has been this way, more or less, since I moved in eleven months ago. I've just never been able to muster the strength to finish unpacking and putting everything in order. Although my logical mind has accepted the fact that life has changed, part of me must continue to believe my current circumstances are just temporary.

Lying on the couch staring at my wading bag and rod cases, I long to lose myself once more on a stream, but the drought warnings for Potter County are proving true. Since returning home four days ago, television newscasts and newspapers have begun dwelling more and more on the need for rain. Reports have filtered in of no water in Loyalhanna and Laurel Hill Creeks. Unless it rains soon, trout fishing will be finished for the year. It probably already is finished. Why can't it be like last year, when rain fell throughout the summer and there was great fishing into August?

Then I remember Tug telling me that bluegills are still spawning at Acme Dam. Normally, they would have finished spawning by mid-June. I decide to take what I can get. Bluegills have been a special love of mine since boyhood. I adore them because their willingness to hit a fly means I don't have to think too much to catch them. Trout often require thought. Sometimes it is wonderful to fish without thinking. Every year I make sure to get in at least a few days of bluegill fishing.

As I climb Chestnut Ridge toward Acme Dam in Westmoreland County, my thoughts drift to anglers who brag about catching fifty or a hundred fish in one day. Since I normally get bored when fishing is too easy, I can only remember posting something near those figures once. It was at a fishing derby when I was a kid of about ten or eleven. My brother and I could do nothing wrong that day. It seemed as if every cast we made ended with another bluegill, until we caught forty-five or forty-eight, I no longer recall the exact total, and Dad said that was enough. He made us clean all those fish, too, which may be part of the reason I am not fascinated by numbers today.

Turning onto County Line Road leading back to Acme Dam, I wonder what it would actually be like to catch a hundred fish in a single day. With the bluegills on their spawning beds, it seems possible. When the dam comes into sight, I think I am going to try. It is 5:30 P.M.

Hurrying down the path on the east side of the lake, I notice plenty of bluegills holding over bright nesting circles of gravel and clay all along the bank. They are within easy casting range—and aggressive, I decide, when three fish from separate beds drive off a pair of perch, then turn on each other. Once my rod is ready, I pull a foam beetle from my vest. I choose the pattern because it worked so well in Potter County. No sooner does it touch the water than I am fast to a bluegill. When the next dozen casts bring only misses, though, I think the hook is too obstructed by the beetle's body for the quick little fish with their small mouths. I change to a little yellow-bodied grasshopper that takes a bass of about eight inches on the first cast. I never thought about bass, but they have moved in close, like the perch, to feed on the nests.

After releasing the bass, I take eight bluegills in rapid succession. Actually, most of the fish are pumpkinseeds, but everybody I know uses the word *bluegill* interchangeably with *panfish*, the category of fish to which bluegills belong. I see no need to change, especially since I like the word *bluegill* better than I do *pumpkinseed, sunfish, panfish,* or *bream.* All eight of the bluegills hit the grasshopper hard, taking it so deep I have to use hemostats to remove the barbless hook and by the eighth fish the grasshopper is little more than a hank of yarn hanging off the hook.

As I exchange the grasshopper for a Humpy, the wind picks up and the action stops. Several fruitless casts lead me to change tactics and stalk the bank for rise forms. My ninth fish follows, another small bass, and quickly after it my tenth, a very large bluegill. Then it starts to sprinkle rain.

Fortunately, the shower lasts only a few moments and with its end come number eleven and number twelve, two more bass, one of them a foot long. They are succeeded by one of the largest bluegills I've caught in years. It is as large as my hand, bright orange, yellow, and glorious blue. I have to pause for a moment to admire it.

Another change in tactics—to fast stripping line that causes the Humpy to race across the surface like some panicky creature worried about being eaten—drives my total up to two dozen. There it stands for about fifteen minutes, and I wonder if I'll reach my goal, but then number twenty-five comes and is rapidly followed by numbers twenty-six and twenty-seven. I seem to be doing best where the waves and slack water meet. Number thirty I miss twice; Thirty-four is another bright fish, almost as pretty as the big one, and number thirty-seven sips the Humpy off the surface. Bluegills are not known for their subtlety, but they sometimes take a fly as delicately as the most discerning trout.

After releasing number forty-four, a fish so fat I can't get my hand around it, I check my watch. It is 7:05. Little more than an hour and a half has passed and I am not yet halfway to my goal. I wonder if I'll make it. Before I know it, though, I am up to fifty-one, which hits a long, beautiful cast, and then fifty-three, which comes from a rise ring. Fifty-four is my first bass in some time, a six-incher. Then, after fifty-six, a bad back cast leaves the Humpy in the weeds and I go back to the grasshopper.

When I miss the next several fish, I pause to check the grass-hopper. Body material is trailing off the hook. The fish are hitting at the material and missing the hook. I trim off the loose yarn and find myself quickly back in business with fifty-seven, fifty-eight, fifty-nine, sixty, sixty-one. Then I begin missing again. I miss sixty-two exactly ten times and don't break the spell until I move down the bank. The movement makes me aware that my back is aching from standing and casting for so long.

Once sixty-two is reached, they come fast once more. Sixty-four and sixty-five explode out of the water, and then before I know it I am up to sixty-nine. My back is really beginning to ache. At number seventy-three, the grasshopper dies. Nothing is left but part of the head and the wings. I put on another grasshop-per and move on to seventy-seven, at which point I suddenly wish it was all over.

With the fun gone, I become lazy. My back cast drops and hangs up in the weeds. My thumb and forefinger hurt from twist-ing out so many hooks. Then at eighty-eight my resolve returns as suddenly as it left. The end is in sight. Ninety is a golden shiner. The vast majority of anglers think of shiners as trash fish, but both Izaak Walton and Theodore Gordon fished for them. This one is beautiful, as brilliant in the fading evening light as a bar of the mineral from which it takes its name.

Anxious to end it all, I hurry up the bank to a series of rise rings, exchange the grasshopper for a Royal Wulff and immedi-ately take ninety-one. Then I miss a full dozen before I notice that the hook on the Royal Wulff is bent. I tie on a moth. Ninety-six, ninety-seven, ninety-eight are all golden shiners that put up good fights, splashing wildly across the surface. I'll never look at the fish in the same way again.

Number ninety-nine is a small bass and number one hundred a dirty-bellied bluegill. It is 8:45 P.M. Three hours and fifteen minutes have passed. My casting arm and shoulder are numb. I wonder how many fishermen actually have caught a hundred fish in one day and thought it fun. Then I take the Royal Wulff with the bent hook and place it in a bush on the edge of the water. I don't know why, but it feels appropriate.

Two days later a slight stiffness remains in my shoulder. My feelings about catching one hundred fish continue mixed. I am glad I did it—now, I can speak with authority when somebody mentions catching one hundred fish—but I doubt very much that I will ever do it again.

Knowing that bluegills are still on their spawning beds and willing to hit, though, makes me think this might be a perfect time to introduce BC to fly fishing. Since she was five years old we've fished for bluegills using worms and spin-casting tackle. Because I've always taken her to places where I knew she could catch fish, she enjoys the sport. And I cherish the opportunity to sit with her on the bank and talk.

Never shy about revealing what is on her mind, she really pours her heart out when we are alone on the water. We talk about birds, plants, animals in the woods, school, disputes with her mother, her friends, things she doesn't understand about the world, and, beginning when she started junior high school, occasionally boys. I tease her that she is my girl and those boys better leave her alone. She smiles shyly, sure I am only teasing. But there actually is a part of me that wants to keep forever the little girl who has made my life so enjoyable.

Often too we laugh when we are fishing. Once she made me laugh so hard, I literally cried. We were camping near State College and one evening decided to walk over to the campground's pond and try our luck. The fishing was slow and BC seemed on the verge of becoming bored when suddenly her bobber dipped under the surface. Assuming bluegill, I told her to pay attention and grab her rod. When she did, the quiet pond exploded in such fury that her mother yelled for me to grab her and everybody else around the pond stopped what they were doing. But none of it phased BC. Her mouth set in determination and the handle of the rod planted in her little belly, she leaned back and fought the fish until she landed it, a fifteen-and-a-half-inch bowfin.

On the phone BC sounds tired and I worry something is wrong. Then she reminds me she spent yesterday at an amusement park. She rode its new roller coaster. It scared her the first time, but then she liked it and rode it another five times. When I tell her the bluegills are biting and ask if she wants to go fishing, she is a little slow to respond until I suggest tying a couple of flies first. She has been after me to teach her how to tie flies for years. Rare is the kid who is not fascinated by the feathers, furs, and colorful yarns of fly tying.

Although I've always answered her questions about the process and have occasionally allowed her to tie a piece of feather or yarn onto one of my flies, I've held out on teaching her how to tie flies because I've never felt she was ready. I wanted her interest to reach a low, steady boil that will continue for a long time and not evaporate like the overheated water of her favorite food, spaghetti. There is nothing to tell me it is at that point today, but I haven't seen her in over a week. I miss her and want us to have a special time together.

When I pick her up, I am a little startled at how tired she appears. Her eyes are squinty and glazed with the far-off stare she gets when exhausted. She obviously gave the park everything she had. But nothing is more resilient than a kid with an opportunity for fun. As we sit down at the vice and work the material onto the hook, her face spreads in a grin so wide her cheeks appear on the verge of bursting. We tie a couple of bushy flies using whatever materials and colors catch our eye, and then she places them in a small plastic box and stares at them with that special intensity of hers that can give a key chain or toy from a box of Cracker Jack the importance of the Hope Diamond. Satisfied with her handiwork, she goes to the refrigerator and fills her plastic travel cup with cola. Then she pulls on her fishing cap with the trout patch on the crown and fly pin on the side, and we head for the car.

On the drive to Acme, the amusement park regains the upper hand and she nods off to sleep, bouncing back to consciousness from time to time when her head drops below a certain point, and then slowly drifting off again, her head falling, falling, falling, until the critical point is past and she springs back eyes wide open. Once she drops too low and stabs herself in the forehead with the straw sticking out of her cup. I move the cup and smile.

When we arrive at the dam, I ask BC how she thinks we'll do. She tells me fine because she has her own flies now and "they are red and brown and cute." I tease her that it sounds like more of her usual bull and she ignores me.

Not wanting to lose her with too much detail on her first try with a fly rod, I rig up an outfit and pull just enough line out to reach fish without having to do any false casting. Too many people become overwhelmed by the details when they are learning how to fly cast. I want it to be fun for her. If it's fun she'll want to learn more.

No bluegill comes on BC's first cast or second or third. Worried that the fish may have finished their spawning and lost their aggressiveness, I take the rod, make several casts to judge the location of the fish and catch two. Then I give her back the rod and a moment later she has her first fish on a fly. It is a large bluegill and I have her hold it up so I can take a picture. Her eyes have that same enthralled stare as when she was examining her flies.

It takes only a few more fish for her to say she likes fly fishing better than bait fishing. When I ask her why, she says: "Because they're all big fish and no little ones." I tell her the flies have nothing to do with the size of the fish, but she is not interested in facts. All she knows is that she is catching fish that fight hard. She is so lost in excitement, in fact, she ignores the surprise pain that comes when she grabs a fish and gets a handful of sharp dorsal fin.

"I don't care," she answers when I ask if she is hurt.

But nothing stays the same for long in a kid's world, and minutes later she is complaining that we've been standing too long in one place and heads off down the shore. I tell her not to go too far, the fish are still in front of us, but it doesn't matter, and when I reach her she is talking to the water. "We don't want a little one. We want a big one," she says when a small bluegill approaches her fly. "Get lost."

Number eleven is a heavy fish that has her shouting "make my day." She was seven or eight years old when she wandered through the living room one evening and heard Clint Eastwood utter the phrase on television. For the longest time afterward, it was her favorite line.

At number eighteen excitement is suddenly replaced with boredom, and seemingly, from the drooping look in her eyes, exhaustion. The adrenaline stirred by the new experience is gone. She wants to catch only two more fish, reach twenty, and quit. She is in such a hurry to end everything that when she doesn't catch two fish within a minute she asks if she can count mine. I tell her that would be cheating. Then a couple of minutes later she has her last two fish, one of them a small bass that leaps free of the water and for an instant brings her back to life.

As we gather up our gear and head for the car the slight sadness that always comes over me when it is time to take her home begins to build. I put my arm around her shoulder as we walk up the path.

"Well, how did you like fly fishing?" I ask.

"It was fun," she says.

"Did you like it better than fishing with worms?"

"Yeah, man!" she says. "That rod makes those fish dance," making me burst into laughter.

Bodines

"Bodines! Bodines! What a queer name for a book! Where under the sun did you run across such a title as that?" So begins *Bodines; or, Camping on the Lycoming,* a book that when it was published by J. B. Lippincott & Company of Philadelphia in 1879 became the first in a long shelf of volumes devoted exclusively to angling in Pennsylvania.

Centered around the village of Bodines on Lycoming Creek in Lycoming County, *Bodines* was written by Dr. Thaddeus Stevens Up de Graff, who was born in Harrisburg on April 12, 1839. No information appears in Up de Graff's obituaries about his mother, but his father was Dr. John J. Up de Graff, who practiced medicine in Lingleston, Dauphin County. He named his son after their family friend Thaddeus Stevens, the abolitionist and father of public school education in Pennsylvania.

As a boy, Up de Graff attended a seminary in Selinsgrove on the Susquehanna River in Snyder County, and then spent five years studying medicine and surgery with his father. Later, he studied at the St. Louis Medical School and the University of Michigan. After graduating from medical school, Up de Graff married Ella Hale of Indianapolis, Indiana, on December 1, 1859, and the couple moved to Olney, Illinois, where he established his first practice. When the Civil War erupted in April 1861, he obtained a commission as a captain and raised a company of men that fought with the Twenty-Sixth Illinois Volunteers in several battles on the southwestern front. In 1862, Up de Graff was wounded at the Battle of Mill Spring, Kentucky, and "was afterward very ill and was compelled to resign."

Once recovered from his wounds, Up de Graff resumed his medical practice in Vincennes, Indiana, and then brought his family back east to Elmira, New York, where his parents had moved from Harrisburg. In Elmira, Up de Graff gained prominence on both the medical and the social fronts. He belonged to numerous social organizations, served on the school board and, in 1865, founded the Elmira Medical and Surgical Institute, the city's first hospital. "A feature of his work there was the free treatment given two days each week to those unable to pay," according to the *Elmira Star-Gazette.*

As a doctor, Up de Graff gained wide renown for his surgical ability involving the eyes and ears. "Patients came to him from every part of the union," according to the *Elmira Daily Advertiser.* "His marvelous skill and his wide reputation are shown in the fact that the books show that he operated in over 800 cases for the removal of cataracts alone."

Up de Graff also discovered a new bacteria and was the first person to prove that human blood corpuscles could be "detected with certainty from that of the dog." In addition, he designed numerous surgical instruments and published a professional medical journal called *Bistoury*. In 1882, he was named a fellow of the Royal Microscopical Society of Great Britain.

Although he grew up on the Susquehanna River, Up de Graff did not become a serious angler until he met Samuel Hamlin, the Elmira dry goods dealer to whom *Bodines* is dedicated. Hamlin retired from business in 1861 after the death of his only son and afterward spent most of his time fishing and hunting. He introduced Up de Graff to Lycoming Creek around 1864, and according to the *Star-Gazette*, "from that time the two annually enjoyed a return to the alluring region of which we read in the fresh, unaffected and interesting 'Bodines.'"

At first, Up de Graff's trips to Lycoming County were relatively short, lasting only a week or so, but by the beginning of the 1870s, they had grown to a month or more, during which time he, Hamlin, and a varying assortment of other friends camped on an island in Lycoming Creek between Grays Run and Pleasant

Stream. The name Bodines comes from John Bodine (or "Squire" Bodine, as Up de Graff refers to him), a settler who had moved to the Lycoming Valley in the 1820s and with whom the doctor and Hamlin often stayed.

Although the *Bodines* book was a success from the beginning, Up de Graff himself never looked upon it as anything but a series of "unpretending sketches" about vacations he spent with friends fishing for trout. What he left, though, was a highly readable record of angling in north-central Pennsylvania when virgin forests still covered most of the land—a record full of fascinating details on equipment and tactics used by anglers just after the Civil War. His observations on aquatic insect life and fish behavior are sometimes incorrect. Nevertheless, he manages to touch a chord of emotion that still resonates within anglers today. He writes of watching caddis flies and mayflies:

> On the high bank, we lie down and peer into the water, through an opera-glass, observing the curious forms of insect life that swarm upon the bottom of the creek. There, we see strange little worm-like creatures, crawling about with bundles of sticks upon their backs, or with a coat of mail, constructed of minute pebbles, glued together in some mysterious manner. This becomes their armor . . . to protect them from the fish particularly the lazy, long-nosed suckers, that are constantly turning them over in order to get a nip at them. Some, bursting their chrysalid shells, float to the surface of the water, rest a moment, pluming their delicate wings, and then take their flight to join the myriads of similar insects flying through the air. To sit down, or, better still, to lie down, and watch these wiggling little creatures transforming themselves into graceful and brilliant flying insects, often rivalling the flowers in gaudy colors, is a diversion of no mean description.

Typical of fly fishermen of the period, Up de Graff and Hamlin normally fished two wet flies across and downstream. Their favorite flies, tied on hook "Nos. 19 and 14," included well-known patterns such as the Black Gnat, Grizzly King, and Queen of the Water, as well as lesser-known creations such as the Great Dun, tied with a mouse-colored body, grayish hackle, long speckled tail, and lead-colored wing, and their own invention the "Hamlin," tied with a black body, black hackle, white wing, and long black tail with a white tip.

To fish the flies, Up de Graff used a tapered, braided linen line and seven-foot-long silkworm gut leader. Modern fly fishermen tend to believe their nineteenth-century counterparts used silk lines or horsehair lines, but the doctor preferred linen because it was lighter and "is delivered more freely through the rings, and does not fray." Also contrary to the opinions of many contemporary anglers, the *Bodines* campers had little use for cane rods. "I wouldn't give a cent for one for our use," one of Up de Graff's friends remarks. "They will do very well for a day or two fishing in fair weather; but just stand them up against a tree, where they take the rain, dew, dampness, for a month, and they will be found soon to lose their elasticity and spring qualities." Even when properly varnished (including once before a trip, twice at the end of the season, and once more at the beginning), cane rods of the time often ended up "as crooked as a ram's horn, and quite as useless." They came with the disadvantage of being unrepairable if broken during a lengthy trip. "You can't sit down and mend it on the stream, as you do your lancewood."

For a reel, Up de Graff preferred a nickel-plated "click reel" because the click "regulates the movement of a reel better than any other device, besides being a merry indicator of the fish's strike." On one occasion, Up de Graff's click reel provided a story no angler would ever be allowed to live down. It happened on Lycoming Creek. Hamlin was sitting on the bank fussing with his leader. The roar of the water kept him from hearing Up de Graff's approach until the doctor was only a step behind him and his line caught in a twig, "giving the reel a sudden rattle just behind his head." Thinking the sound a rattlesnake, Hamlin instantly jumped into the stream, and then turned only to confront his friend, whom he blasted for having a reel that was the "best imitation of that venomous reptile I ever had the misfortune of listening to."

Even more than its views on equipment and tactics, *Bodines*'s value lies in its description of the country and of the people who lived in north-central Pennsylvania after the Civil War. Many of the names in the book remain familiar today—Slate Run, Young Womans Creek, Oleana, Trout Run, Pine Creek, Germania, Cross

Fork Creek, Kettle Creek. He writes of the area: "The country is very wild and rugged; not a house is seen for miles, as you fish up and down the stream. Wild animals are constantly encountered. Deer meet you on the stream and stare you out of countenance, and bears and wild-cats scramble out of the way as you pass along. No more delightful waters for fly-fishing can be found in the State; the fish are bountiful and of large size."

Wilderness regions are known for attracting characters and misanthropes of all sorts, and the situation was no different in the 1870s. *Bodines* is full of portraits of the people Up de Graff encountered on his fishing trips. Some of them are touching, others amusing, and a few sad. At what is now Ole Bull State Park on Kettle Creek, Up de Graff met "Mr. Anderson," the original secretary of the utopian colony that the Norwegian violinist Ole Bull had founded along the stream in the 1850s.

Among the most memorable characters in the book is Shorty, perhaps the most colorful of all the people Up de Graff encountered along northern Pennsylvania streams. Shorty was a market fisherman "as well known, by name at least, as any denizen of the Lycoming valley." Up de Graff was so taken with the backwoods character he devotes an entire chapter to him. He does so even though he acknowledges that, without Shorty, "the streams of the Lycoming region would be far more populous of trout."

Up de Graff and Hamlin were fishing Pleasant Stream when Shorty first appeared. Hamlin had just hooked a fish that was giving him a hard time. It tangled the angler in his leader, ran between both his and Up de Graff's legs, and generally was doing everything possible to avoid capture. When Up de Graff went to net the trout, it jumped clear of his net and finally threw the hook. Then a voice spoke in the background.

"I knew you'd lose 'im. I caught one bigger'n him, over on Pine Creek, once, and he mixed three of us up just as this'un did you fellers, and jumped clean over my head and knocked my boy down."

Looking up, Up de Graff and Hamlin found themselves staring at a short man of about fifty, with shaggy, unkempt hair and beard, and his grin showing a mouthful of tobacco stained teeth.

He wore a black coat, threadbare, and abundantly patched, while his trousers (what was left of them) exposed a once

white shirt, from front and rear, and a well-bronzed skin at
the knees. This uniform was topped out with a black
slouch hat, profusely ornamented with artificial flies,
which seemed to have been collected from the back leaves
of the fly-books of all fishermen who had visited this
stream for the past two years. On his shoulder rested a pole
that evidently had been cut in the woods, while in his hand
was an old, six-quart tin pail, covered with a dirty rag, a
hole cut in the centre, through which to thrust his trout.

Sensing a free meal when Up de Graff and Hamlin walked out of
the stream carrying a creel full of fish, Shorty invited them to use
his fire. While the two worked cleaning their trout, Shorty told
them he had fished local streams for twenty years, knew every
rock and stump in them, and took all of his trout on flies. As
proof of his prowess, he opened his pail to reveal it two-thirds
full of trout from one to twelve inches long, which he had caught
in less than an hour, "four and five at a time."

"Four and five at a time!" exclaimed Hamlin, who had just
lighted his pipe and was holding a burning ember aloft, to catch
the direction of the wind. "Why, man, how many flies do you
usually attach to a leader?"

"Oh, sometimes ten and sometimes twelve, accordin' as to
how they're bitin'."

Pointing to a nearby pool, Shorty revealed another of his
fishing methods. He said that one day, some years earlier, he had
counted "one hundred and twenty-two busters, every one on 'em
weighing mor'n a pound," lying in the pool. Determined to catch
all of them, Shorty cut branches and threw them into the pool so
no passing fisherman would spot the trout. Then he began feeding them chicken entrails every morning and evening. The trout
became "mighty fond of 'em" and would gather when they saw
Shorty approaching.

Once the trout came to expect the feedings, Shorty led them
into the next pool by throwing the chicken entrails into the water a little farther upstream every day. At the mouth of the pool
he built a brush dam with a board he could lower to shut off the
water. Once the fish were packed tight in the pool, he dropped
the board and shut off the water, and then "picked out every
blessed one on 'em with my bare hands!"

When Up de Graff complained that catching fish in such a manner did not seem to be much fun, Shorty responded by pointing out "that's all werry well for you fellers what's got lots o' money and nuthin' to do to talk about. But when a poor feller like me, with a big family a-dependin' on 'im for sumthin to eat it's a different story."

Warned that taking so many fish would soon ruin the fishing, Shorty replied that he often sold his fish to city anglers. "Yes, you city fellers all says that; but I allers notices that you never throws 'em in yourselves."

When Up de Graff protested that no true sportsman would do such a thing, Shorty replied: "Well, I dunno: it 'pears to me what you calls yer true uns never comes this way, then."

After relating a tale about a giant trout that swallowed a thirty-inch eel, Shorty inquired if Up de Graff and Hamlin might like to buy some fish, which sent Hamlin into a fit. Shorty quickly apologized, saying he did not think they would buy them because he did not see a flask among their gear, but he thought they might have hidden it.

"Flask! Flask! What's that got to do with it?" Hamlin inquired.

"Oh, a heap. I allers notices that them feller whot carry their baskets under one arm and a flask a-hangin' under t'other have more luck a-drinkin' than they do a-ketchin' ov fish."

Up de Graff died on August 3, 1885, after "several years of delicate health" and a long illness. He was forty-six years old. Following services in Elmira, his body was taken by train to Lancaster where it was cremated and then returned to Elmira for interment. Hamlin continued fishing at Bodines. He died in Elmira in 1908.

Wild Trout

By the end of June, following a couple of weeks of daily ninety-degree-plus temperatures, the governor's office confirms what every angler has been saying for a month. The office issues a drought warning for counties in the central part of the state. The lieutenant governor says the situation is serious, but not critical. In the next breath he reports that the Susquehanna River is at its lowest level in ninety years, and that stream and groundwater levels are approaching their lowest levels of the twentieth century. A task force has been formed.

Near the end of July, a drought emergency is declared in thirty-nine counties. The order bans open fires, watering lawns, filling swimming pools, washing cars, and running ornamental fountains. Rainfall for the thirty-nine counties is averaging 6.5 inches below normal and stream flow 70 percent below normal. Western Pennsylvania is faring a little better than the center of the state. The heavier normal rains of spring are still in the ground. Precipitation totals for the year are down by more than an inch and a half. It won't be long before western Pennsylvania is in the same condition as the center of the state. It is tough to let go of a season that has meant so much to me. I call Jan Caveney to see if we can sneak in a day of wild rainbow fishing.

Jan is a waterways conservation officer with the Fish and Boat Commission. I felt an immediate affinity for him when we first met a few years ago at a Trout Unlimited banquet. The link was angling literature. Jan knew of my love for fishing books through my writing. He told me he was a collector. The remark set off a conversation that lasted throughout the banquet. When I visited his home a few weeks later to browse through his collection of more than twelve hundred volumes, his wife, Betty, could only smile and shake her head as if she was watching two children intently at play.

Along with collecting books, Jan also collects streams. He originally moved to Pennsylvania from his boyhood home in Bethesda, Maryland, to be closer to the state's famous trout waters, and to try for a job with the Fish and Boat Commission. Even before moving, he had made numerous fishing trips to the state, ferreting out well-known and unusual waters. It was during one of our typical lengthy conversations that he mentioned two streams in the Laurel Highlands with reproducing populations of rainbow trout and promised to take me there.

"I love showing people new streams in their own area," he teased.

By the time I enter the used bookstore in the Laurel Highlands where we've agreed to meet, Jan has already checked the shelves for angling works. He quickly informs me there is nothing of interest. Then we head outside, transfer gear from my car to his four-wheel-drive, and head off into the mountains. The first stream we stop at is ringed by private property, but Jan knows the owner of a stretch of water. When we knock on his door, he greets Jan with a laugh of recognition and tells us the stream is down.

"We need rain bad," he adds, echoing a refrain now heard everywhere. Then he waves us off, telling us to enjoy ourselves while he finishes a chore.

The water we have permission to fish is only about one hundred yards long, so we separate. Jan starts at the house, and I head downstream. After nearly two months without fishing, I am anxious to wet a line. But when I emerge from the rhododendron, I am stopped cold. The stream is practically empty. Even the holes look as if they can be measured with a ruler.

For a moment, all I can do is stare at the exposed rocks, dry mud, and barely trickling current. I wonder if we should be fishing at all. But my need to be on a stream is strong. I rationalize that we are going to release the fish, and then bend down and touch the water. The temperature seems good. At least, it feels good. I have no way of knowing for sure because I still haven't replaced the thermometer that turned up broken on my first trip of the season. I make another mental note to do so.

The effects of my two-month layoff quickly become apparent as I frighten fish after fish in the low, mirror-image water. Jan has not done much better, I find out when I reach him. He has taken only a couple of fish, both of them brook trout. Then, as we talk, he hooks a rainbow. We know instinctively it is a rainbow by the way it rockets out of the water higher and faster than any brookie that's ever lived. It moves so fast Jan can't control the action even with the eight-and-a-half-foot rod he likes to use to drab his fly on tiny streams. On its third jump, the fish lands hard on a rock, leaving Jan worried its spine is broken. He gently lifts the stunned trout, an iridescent six-inch slash of red, green, and silver.

"They're beautiful," I say.

"I didn't think he'd come out of the water like that," Jan replies with a troubled voice. Then he releases the fish and we watch as it swims off. Hopefully, it will survive, but there is no way of knowing. We watch the water for a few moments to see if it surfaces belly up. When it doesn't, we separate again.

In the long pool below the house, my personal drought breaks with a brookie of about four inches. I follow this up with another brookie, and then miss a couple more. By the time I reach Jan again his total has climbed to four fish, but they are all brookies. No more rainbows. I tell him I want to try the water at the lower end of the stretch once more and then hurry down the road and through the rhododendron to find a fish rising close to the root tangle of a small hemlock.

Crouching so low my back aches, I cross the stream to an open spot and send out a twenty-foot cast, twelve feet of which lands on dry land, to hook the only leaf on the pool. Not wanting to disturb the water, I wait for the leaf to float closer, and then lift the fly free and send another cast toward the roots. Bam! Like a beam of light, my line zips across the pool as I run toward the water stripping in slack. The fish does not jump, but its quickness makes me think it is a rainbow.

"All right," I tell myself happily when I finally see it. "My first wild Pennsylvania rainbow!"

The statement is more emotion than fact. I've caught the wild rainbows in Falling Spring Run, but they are there by plan. The rainbows in the Laurel Highlands are a marvelous accident, a monument to survival. Admiring the flashing red sides of the tiny trout, maybe seven inches, I keep it out of the water longer than I normally would. Then I twist the barbless hook from its lip, let it slip back into the pool where it instantly disappears, and I head off to find Jan. When I tell Jan what happened, he smiles the contented smile of an angler who has just widened another fisherman's world, and then suggests it is time to move on. "We've bored these fish enough," he says.

Like the brown trout, the rainbow trout is a transplant to Pennsylvania. The first hatching of rainbow eggs for stocking purposes occurred in 1870, when the California Acclimatization Society took eggs from waters draining into San Francisco Bay and hatched them in the basement of San Francisco City Hall and on the Berkeley campus of the University of California. The first recorded shipment of rainbow eggs out of California was made in 1875 to Seth Green's Caledonia, New York, hatchery. It involved some five hundred eggs.

Enthusiasm for "California brook trout," or "California mountain trout" as the species was known in the nineteenth century, was high from the beginning. The Fish Commission first stocked rainbow from California's McCloud River in Pennsylvania in 1879 and followed up that stocking with several others. By 1886, interest in the rainbow had begun to wane, though, mainly because the fish disappeared almost as soon as it was stocked. Fish culturists of the time were not aware of the rainbow's migratory habits. "Placed in waters apparently suitable," the Fish Commission's 1895 report states, "they often entirely disappeared almost immediately to turn up in another creek some distance away."

Another reason the rainbows almost immediately disappeared was because they were often stocked in waters that were entirely unsuitable for them. The Fish Commission's 1895 report tells the story:

Finding the rainbow trout was abundant and indigenous in streams of a very warm climate, the government authorities . . . without giving the matter close attention, arrived to the conclusion that this fish would thrive in waters of higher temperature than the eastern brook trout. . . . The result was that as soon as the first lot of fry were ready for distribution, there was a widespread and great demand for them. Many of these little fish were placed in streams the water of which was as high as 70 degrees, and in which there was not even the compensation of aeration by extreme rapidity of flow. To the surprise of those who stocked streams of this character and even many waters in which speckled trout lived, there were no returns, and a few months after the planting there was not a vestige of the fish. . . . At length the secret was discovered.

In taking the climate of California as a basis for the expression of belief that the rainbow trout would thrive in water of a higher temperature than the eastern brook trout, the authorities made a grave error. While the climate was much warmer, the water in which the rainbow trout had their original home were of the coldest and purest character, having their sources in the perpetual ice and snows of the mountains.

By 1900, problems facing the rainbow in Pennsylvania cut production of the trout to next to nothing. In 1914, entries for it in the official report cease altogether. Fish Commissioner Oliver Diebler tried to resurrect interest in the fish after World War I, but the attempt failed and the rainbow settled back into obscurity again. There it remained until 1933, when a Centre County angler, Earl Kline, obtained some fingerling rainbows from the federal government and planted them in tributaries of Spring Creek. By the following spring, the fish had grown to ten or twelve inches and had spread over a good portion of the stream. The trout reached fifteen inches by the end of the summer, and "fishing was the best in the history of the stream."

Drawing hope from Kline's experiment, the Fish Commission in the mid-1930s once more decided to attempt the stocking of rainbows. A domestic stock of rainbows was obtained from a private hatchery in New England and blended with a strain from the federal fish hatchery at Wytheville, Virginia. The resulting strain was less prone to migrate than the original fish brought east in the 1870s. More important, the commission also switched from stocking fingerlings to stocking yearling fish.

Remnants of early stockings remain in a small number of streams scattered around the state. The rainbows Jan found in the Laurel Highlands are said to be the survivors of a private stocking that took place in 1910. How true this might be nobody knows. Fish Commission records show that rainbow fry were delivered to the area before that date, so they could be part of an even earlier attempt to establish "California mountain trout" in the area. They also could be from later stockings.

The second stream we are exploring is farther up the mountain and in the woods, which immediately has me excited. The first stream was fun, but wild fish belong in the woods, in country that at least carries an illusion of wilderness, even if a highway is only a couple of hundred yards away. My anticipation is quickly rewarded at the first pool. I miss two fish. Then two more strike at my Renegade in the next pool. They are fish that are probably too small to take my fly. Finally I hook the fifth, a brookie.

From the number of strikes, it seems clear this stream holds more fish than the first one. My hunch proves true as I work my way up the mountain, taking or missing fish in every pool, but they are all brookies. It is not until I reach a deep hole on a bend under a high bank that I take a rainbow. It rockets from the junction of two currents, leaping once, twice, three times, and then digging deep for a tree limb. The difference in strength between the rainbow and brookies is remarkable. The rainbows put a real bend in my rod.

"I love this," I find myself saying, when the fish finally surrenders, startling me with its size. I mark its length on my rod, and then release it and measure the distance. Ten inches. The day suddenly feels complete. I am ready to call it quits, get something to eat. I won't do better. But Jan is nowhere in sight. I decide to check out more of the stream.

My curiosity pays off a few minutes later, when I look up to find myself surrounded by bright Yellow and Lime Sallies. The little stoneflies rise and flutter about me like fairies in a Disney movie. A fish rises from the pool and snatches one out of midair, the act adding to the scene. Backing up onto a rock, I sit down and stretch out my legs. The ache in my knees and back reminds me I've reached forty. I check my watch and find we've been fishing for six hours. Then another fish clears the water, after one of the stoneflies. I don't know if it is lucky, but I certainly feel so for having seen its stab at dinner. I wonder what the drought eventually will do to the stream, if fish will continue to survive. I know I'm on my last fishing trip of the summer.

The thought of my season ending stirs a real sadness. I want to watch more flies dance above quiet pools, listen to the birds calling through the rustling leaves, smell the rich, dark earth that surrounds mountain streams, and be startled by an unexpected rise. But to continue would be pure selfishness. The fish need to be left alone.

Sage from Pittsburgh

⌒~∽

No name is more hallowed in American fly-fishing history than that of Theodore Gordon. Paul Schullery in *American Fly Fishing* writes that, rightly or wrongly, Gordon "has become the central figure in the history of American fly fishing. . . . It is from Gordon that the modern tradition is most often said to flow. . . . He is unrivaled in his importance as a symbol." Few names are as closely associated with a particular region as Gordon's name is to the Catskill Mountains of New York. The image of him sitting alone in his cabin above the Neversink River during the long winter months, inventing the familiar Catskill style of dry fly, is one of the most romantic in all of angling literature.

Certainly there is no refuting the importance of the Catskills in Gordon's life, work, and legend. What seems to be overlooked is his connection to Pennsylvania and its influence on him. For not only did he come from Pittsburgh, but he caught his first trout in the Cumberland Valley and was at least partially inspired to learn fly fishing after watching anglers on Big Spring, Cumberland County, and to study entomology after encountering the "highly educated" trout of Spring Creek, Centre County.

The godfather of American fly fishing, as he has been called, was born in Pittsburgh on September 18, 1854. His mother was Fanny Jones, who also was born in the city. Orphaned at an early age, Fanny had been raised by an aunt and uncle in Mobile, Alabama, where she met and, in 1850, married Theodore Gordon Senior, a member of an old New York City family who had gone south for his health. The couple moved to Pittsburgh some time before Gordon's birth and then returned to Mobile, where the elder Gordon contracted malaria and died at the age of thirty.

With feelings against Northerners running high, and her money in short supply, Fanny and her son returned to Pittsburgh in 1860, where they lived with her sister Anna and her husband, Joseph Spencer, a well-to-do merchant. "Here the six-year-old Theodore spent what were undoubtedly the happiest years of his life," writes Sparse Grey Hackle in *Fishless Days, Angling Nights*, "for the Spencers had a summer farm at Carlisle, Pennsylvania, in an area that was then a paradise for fishermen and hunters." In the company of his cousins Charles and Robert Spencer, Gordon "roamed the woods and fields from dawn to dark," Hackle notes. "In those years he gained the knowledge of shooting and fishing and the great love of nature and passion for the outdoors that remained with him as long as he lived."

Gordon himself would later write lovingly of his time in Carlisle and on the Bonny Brook section of Letort Spring Run, where he took his first trout. Like countless boys before and since, this central figure of American fly fishing caught his first trout on a worm. His companion was a local angler named Docky Noble who favored worms scented with assafetida (a gum resin that smells like garlic). Docky prepared the worms by placing them in a dirty sock with a piece of the resin, a combination that "perfumed the whole house."

Bonny Brook also was where a thirteen-year-old Gordon encountered his first *big* trout, a fish that broke his first good fly rod, a rod he had scrimped and saved a long time to buy. It happened when he drifted a worm under a hollow bank.

> I was not conscious of a bite, but on trying to withdrawal the line found it was held fast. Forgetting my delicate tackle, a vigorous pull was given, the rod bent double and a large trout was drawn to the surface. Becoming wildly excited, I endeavored to haul the fish out on the narrow margin between the fence and the pool; the trout was actually drawn half out of the water; when the rod broke in two places, the trout disappeared and before I could gain

control of the line, freed himself from the hook. I could
have lifted up my voice and wept; my feelings can hardly be
realized. My legs were weak, and a sensation of utter
goneness and woe possessed me. To break my beautiful
new rod was a frightful misfortune, but to lose that trout
was a calamity indeed. I had never seen such a trout; it was
at least twelve inches long and may have weighed three-
quarters of a pound.

Winters in Pittsburgh being extremely damp and Gordon a
very frail child prone to terrible colds and related ailments, Fanny
became distraught about her son's health and overly protective.
She first curtailed his school attendance to keep him away from
other children who might be carrying a disease, and then his summer activities in the outdoors. The restrictions frustrated the
young Gordon, made him withdraw into himself, turn moody
and sullen. People who knew him in later life often described
him as being an unpleasant and cranky person who was almost
obsessive about his privacy and apparently uncaring about his
mother. He often complained bitterly about her being a burden,
but at the same time he remained financially and emotionally
dependent on her most of his life. Today, he shares her burial
crypt in New York City.

Soon after the Civil War ended, Fanny headed south again
with her son to escape Pittsburgh's climate. Little is known about
Gordon's life in the South until 1880, when he and his mother
appeared in Savannah, Georgia. There Gordon worked as a book-
keeper and in the securities business, while the family's fortunes
steadily declined.

After the second move south, Gordon would never again live
in Pennsylvania, but he would continue to visit and fish in the
state for most of his life. He regularly mentions it in his articles
for the *Fishing Gazette* in England and *Forest & Stream* in New
York. He was particularly fond of Big Spring in Cumberland
County, where he received, if not his first, then one of his earliest
exposures to fly fishing, of sorts:

The native anglers made their own rods of two pieces of
hickory, lashed or ferruled together and painted green,
usually they cared not for a reel, but wound the surplus line

in one place on the rod, carrying it from that point and hitching it at the extreme tip. As a rule they used but one fly, and cast about 35 ft. to 40 ft. When a trout rose and was hooked the rod was dropped into the hollow of the left arm, and the fish was played and landed by hand. . . . As my first experience was gained by the side of one of these old fish-hawks, I very naturally imitated him and fished in the same way until I learned better.

Clinton County's Young Womans Creek and Centre County's Spring Creek each played a role in one of Gordon's most memorable fishing trips, an outing that he would recall periodically throughout his life. The trip occurred in either 1872 or 1873. Gordon heard a conductor on the Pennsylvania Railroad brag about the great fishing on Young Womans Creek, and he decided to visit it with two friends. Arriving in the evening, the trio took a room in a lumberman's boardinghouse and awoke the next morning to have their excitement dampened almost immediately. "In the morning we learned that there was no fishing until you went ten miles up stream, and that the lumbermen were skinning every bit of lumber," he would write his friend, Roy Steenrod, years later. "Also that there was no fly-fishing until July."

Having traveled three hundred miles to the stream (he apparently was living somewhere in the South), Gordon and his friends were determined to fish, so they made the ten-mile trip up Young Womans Creek, where, after hours of casting, one member of the party managed to catch a half-pound trout that broke his rod. When a Philadelphia angler he met along the stream confirmed there was no fly fishing until July, Gordon accepted his offer of a few worms and eventually caught eleven fish in a pool thick with debris from the lumbering going on in the area. Realizing it was useless to continue fishing, the trio returned to their hotel, ate the dozen trout they had caught for dinner, and took a late train for Lock Haven. There they found a hotel room and the next morning learned about Spring Creek in Bellefonte. The hotel owner said the stream flowed right through the center of town and contained a lot of trout.

I braced up and thanked him. Hope returned but at breakfast I could do nothing with the two other boys. They were bound to go home and home they went. I on the contrary took the branch railroad up to Bellefonte. Found everything as described by the kind landlord. Had a lovely room, 11 waiters, and excellent meals any time I wanted them. Stayed a week and never had a better time. One day I killed 40 trout but none over 1 lb. (They had me described and my fishing in the paper.)

Gordon points to his experiences on Spring Creek as one of the reasons he began to study entomology. He became aware of the importance of matching the hatch when he was fishing with a local angler. The two men reached a shallow mill dam full of rising fish to which they cast and cast without luck. "Finally, in an old envelope in the pocket of his [fly] book, my friend found a small straw-colored fly closely approximating the fly at which the trout were rising. He put it on, and in half an hour or a little over caught 42 trout. He had only one fly of the kind, so I was forced to play audience, nothing that I could offer being tempting to the fish." Later in the week, Gordon had a similar experience with a dark fly:

> I was fishing with three flies on my leader, and the middle fly happened to be nearest the natural. It had a very thin body of silk, and fishing quite a short line over a deep channel under sheltering willows, I could see the trout rise and take this fly between the two others. After some hours the fly was literally chewed up, and I substituted another, which I thought was very nearly the same. The body was a little lighter and was made of mohair instead of silk. It proved to be entirely useless, and I was forced to put on the mangled remains of the old fly, when I again began to kill fish.

Spring Creek was on Gordon's mind even as he lay dying. In a letter to Steenrod dated March 7, 1915, less than two months before his death, Gordon wrote excitedly about receiving a letter from a "real angler at Bellefonte." He had been trying to correspond with the man for ten years. "Now I know why I got no replies. In such a large town there are a great number of local anglers who are jealous of strangers, and want to keep all foreign fishermen from taking their trout." He told Steenrod: "There are plenty of native trout within 20 miles. One stream 18 miles out he describes as a fisherman's paradise. . . . It is very large and flows between high mountains. A favorite place to camp out in summer. I had such a delightful week at Bellefonte when I was 18 or 19 years old. Good hotel, everybody kind, and lots of very shy trout." It is tempting to think that the "fisherman's paradise" Gordon mentions in his letter became Fisherman's Paradise, the famous experiment in fisheries management located on Spring Creek, but the distance of eighteen miles that Gordon gives places his secret stream too far away. Possibly it was Penns Creek.

Suffering terribly with swollen feet from years of wading wet in icy mountain streams, Gordon died at the age of sixty on May 1, 1915, in the Catskill village of Bradley, Sullivan County, New York. Up to three days before his death he was still writing friends inquiring about their fishing luck, talking tackle and angling books, and remembering the streams in his life. The first of which were in Pennsylvania.

Holding Water

It wasn't a twenty-three-pound grasshopper that drove me to the water that afternoon. Neither was it the morning news, nor a dull, vacant gnawing inside. The world, in fact, seemed pretty good. Better than it had been for a long time. Work was steady, and I finally had accepted it was time to move on. It might sound absurd to people who aren't anglers, but I'm certain much of the credit for the turnaround belongs to fishing. A sense of confidence and stability, even happiness, has grown in me, from my time spent on the water. Fish have once again shown me my place in the world—the insignificance of human problems in the greater scheme of things.

By October 25, the day when the need to be back on the water strikes me, almost two and a half months have passed since the wild rainbow trip with Jan. The fountain at Point State Park in Pittsburgh has been turned off since mid-August. Rainfall for the year is eight inches below normal. It is going to take a lot of snow and a wet spring to get things back to normal, we are constantly being told by the weather people. I have no idea what Dunbar Creek will look like as I turn onto the gravel road that leads back through State Game Lands 51.

My first glimpse of the water through the trees shows a trickle of a stream, choked with a bright quilt of red, yellow, brown, green leaves. I see my fly picking up leaves on every cast. A compact car appears, parked in an opening alongside the road. I wonder if its owner is fishing or grouse hunting, or maybe bow hunting for deer. The seasons have mixed together. Opening day of the rifle buck season is only a month away. It is almost time for *Jeremiah Johnson*. Every fall since I've owned a VCR, I've watched that Robert Redford movie for inspiration as deer season approaches. The first time I saw it was in a theater during college. It made me want to move to the mountains. But the life of the free mountain man lasted only a few years before John Jacob Astor's American Fur Company took over and the beaver were gone. That life wasn't what it first seems to be either.

About halfway down the road to the parking lot at the end, a beat-up red flatbed passes me in the opposite direction. Its occupants, three bearded men in their thirties, are all wearing baseball caps with various insignia on the front. They nod as we pass and I can see fishing rods hanging across the back window. Then out of the rhododendron steps a gray-haired gentleman smoking a pipe. I guess he is the owner of the compact car. He nods and waves. There is something obviously content about him. I have seen the same contentment many times in older men alone on the water after the crowds have gone home.

Unlike my first trip to Dunbar during the stocking frenzy, the parking lot at the end of the road is empty of vehicles. Pulling to a stop under a yellow-leafed birch, I sit and enjoy the quiet for a moment, then get out and look at the sky. It is an absolutely cloudless blue, bright and endless, a sky that could have been the inspiration for the word *heaven*.

With the sky comes that sweet, rotting, musky smell of rich earth that is one of the reasons fall is my favorite time of the year. Once when I was searching for bald eagles at Pymatuning Reservoir in Crawford County with a biologist from the Game Commission, we encountered that smell and went off looking for its source. We might as well have tried to capture the past. Every time we thought we were close, it faded away in another direction. The biologist kept repeating: "I know that smell, I know that smell." In the end, neither his training nor our memories could pin it down.

Once my boots are on and my rod rigged, I head across the road to the pool with the jack dam. The bright sun coming through the yellow leaves paints the stream in a golden glow that reveals several trout circulating through the pool. There is no water coming over the top of the dam; its boards are so dry vandals have spray painted them with graffiti, but enough water is seeping out from between the cracks to push the leaves back a few yards from the dam. Seeing five or six fish moving back and forth through the clear water, I think for the first time I actually might catch a trout.

As I stare at the pool, the old gentleman with the pipe drives past in the compact car and waves again. I return his greeting, and then out of the corner of my eye glimpse a dark movement. I turn to find a mink slinking from rock to rock up the opposite bank. The mink is the first I've encountered on a trout stream in probably a decade. I watch as it bounds, sleek, graceful, silent, along the bank, pausing every so often to stare down into the shallow pools and pockets. It does not see me against a tree. I think it probably has been feeding well in the low water, and I half hope to see it catch a trout, but instead it disappears like a shadow into the brush along the bank.

Once the mink is gone, I slip down to the tail of the pool and (I still haven't replaced my broken thermometer) stick my hand into the water to test the temperature. It is surprisingly cool, somewhere in the mid-sixties I'd guess. I tie on a black foam beetle.

Alerted by the plop of a beetle on the surface, trout will often react by striking. This is exactly what happens. Except three fish rise simultaneously and scare each other off. The same thing happens on my second cast. I think the fish must be starving. On the third cast a single trout rises, puts its nose on the beetle, starts to turn away, thinks better, swings back, and hits. I am slow, dreamy, and I miss it. It is not until my sixth cast that everything falls into place and I come up with a nearly black brookie that reminds me of the dark brookie I caught on Dunbar during the stocking frenzy. Although the fish doesn't look emaciated, it puts up such a weak fight it has to be stressed. A few casts later, I hook another brookie. This one has the large head and shrunken body of a starving fish. Although death in the fall and winter is the frequent fate of stocked trout, the sight always saddens me. After releasing the trout, I decide to give the fish in the pool a break and reel in my line.

The streambed above the jack dam is so low and empty of water that with a little care a person could walk it without getting wet feet. I try it myself until I find a comfortable-looking rock where I sit down to watch the water and feel the air. Weather reports have forecast a high of seventy-eight degrees. There aren't very many days like this left in the year. I close my eyes and feel the breeze on my face. The strange muskiness returns. I inhale it deeply and for a moment think about again trying to search out the sources. But I decide it is enough to simply sit on the water one last time and listen.

Works Cited

Allen, Bill. *The Snakes of Pennsylvania.*

American Turf Register and Sporting Magazine.

Berners, Dame Juliana. *The Treatyse of Fysshynge wyth an Angle.* Edinburgh, 1885.

Bethune, Reverend George Washington, ed. *The Compleat Angler.* 1847.

Bridge, James Howard. *The Inside History of the Carnegie Steel Company: A Romance of Millions.* 1903; rpt. New York, 1972.

Brookes, Richard. *The Art of Angling.* Britain, 1740.

Carnegie, Andrew. *Triumphant Democracy.* 1886; rpt. New York, 1933.

Cooper, Dr. Edwin. *Fishes of Pennsylvania.* University Park, Pa., 1983.

Dunlap's Pennsylvania Packet. Ca. 1770.

Elmira Daily Advertiser.

Elmira Star-Gazette.

Erlich, Paul R. *The Population Bomb.* 1968; rpt. River City, Mass., 1975.

Fishing Gazette. England.

Forest & Stream. New York.

Fox, Charles K. *Rising Trout.* New York, 1978.

———. *This Wonderful World of Trout.*

Gibson, George. *American Turf Register and Sporting Magazine.*

Hackle, Sparse Grey [Alfred Miller]. *Fishless Days, Angling Nights.* 1971; rpt. Piscataway, N.J., 1983.

———. "Those Pennsylvania Boys."

Hallock, Charles, ed. *Forest and Stream.*

Hariot, Thomas. *A briefe and true report of the new found land of Virginia.* London, 1588.

Harrison, Marjorie Butler. *Pennsylvania Descendants of Thomas Norris of Maryland: 1630–1959.*

Henkin, Harmon. *Fly Tackle: A Guide to the Tools of the Trade.* Philadelphia, 1976.

Henshall, James. *Book of the Black Bass.*

Hewitt, Edward R. *A Trout and Salmon Fisherman for Seventy-Five Years.*

Jefferson, Joseph. *Rip Van Winkle.* New York, 1895.

Johnson, C. B. *Letters from the British Settlement in Pennsylvania.* 1819.

Keane, Martin. *Classic Rods and Rodmakers.* New York, 1976.

Kinney, Harry. *The Story of a Ghost Town.*

Lose, Charles. *The Vanishing Trout.* 1928; rpt. Altoona, Pa., 1931.

Malone, E. J. *Irish Trout and Salmon Flies.*

Marinaro, Vincent C. *In the Ring of the Rise.* New York, 1976.

———. *A Modern Dry-Fly Code.*

Mather, Fred. *My Angling Friends.* 1901.

Medve, Richard, and Mary Lee. *Edible Wild Plants of Pennsylvania and Neighboring States.* University Park, Pa., 1990.

Middleton, Harry. *The Earth Is Enough.* New York, 1989.

Miller, Alfred. *See* Hackle, Sparse Grey.

Monnett, John *Cutthroats and Campfires.*

Norris, Thaddeus. *The American Angler's Book: Embracing the Natural History of Sporting Fish, and the Art of Taking Them.* Philadelphia, 1864.

———. *American Fish Culture.*

Outdoors Unlimited (monthly newsletter of the Outdoor Writers Association of America).

Parkman, Francis. *The Jesuits in North America in the Seventeenth Century.* 1867; rpt. Williamstown, Mass., 1970.

Pennsylvania Game News.

Pennsylvania Gazette.

Pennsylvania Magazine of History and Biography. Manuscript published in 1974 edition.

Peterson, Edwin. *No Life So Happy.* New York, 1940.

———. *Penn's Wood West.* Pittsburgh, 1958.

Pinchot, Gifford. *Just Fishing Talk.* Harrisburg, 1993.

———. *Let's Go Fishing.*

Roberts, Thomas. *Memoirs of John Bannister Gibson: Late Chief of Justice of Pennsylvania.* Pittsburgh, 1890.

Roosevelt, Robert Barnwell. *Game Fish of the Northern States of America and British Provinces.* New York, 1862.

Schullery, Paul. *American Fly Fishing.* New York, 1987.

Schwiebert, Ernest George. *Trout.* New York, 1983.

Scott, Genio. *Fishing in American Waters.* 1869; rpt. Seacacus, N.J., 1989.

Shoemaker, Henry. *Black Forest Souvenirs.* Reading, Pa., 1914.

Slaymaker, S. R. *The Fly Fishers Club of Harrisburg*.

Tome, Philip. *Pioneer Life*. Baltimore, 1854.

Up de Graff, Thaddeus Stevens. *Bodines; Or, Camping on the Lycoming*. Philadelphia: J. B. Lippincott, 1879.

Walton, Sir Izaak. *The Compleat Angler*. 1906; rpt. New York, 1965.

Wetherell, W. D. *Upland Stream*. Boston, 1991.

Index